MARRIAGE RX

Marriage Rx

Prescription for a Radical Marriage

By

Calvin & Julie Tadema - Dan & Jody Mayhew

two worlds press

To the bride.
May the joy of the Lord be hers
as she makes herself ready for
the day of her wedding.

Contents

Preface

This book was written because of a near-calamity. Our friends, married nearly 40 years, said they were through, finished, tired of trying to make it work. They were getting a divorce.

We were stunned. Worse, we were indignant as we prepared to sit by and watch another couple crash and burn. We were deeply grieved that this family was going to endure yet another tragedy—they had already lost their oldest son in Iraq.

But, wait a minute. Did we have to just watch it happen? Wasn't there something we could do? You bet there was. We told them *they were not* getting a divorce; they were going to survive their present difficulties and we were going to come alongside to help.

What was the result? They made it through. Not only did they survive, it could be said that they are thriving. Moreover, they helped us all see how married couples desperately need a clearer understanding of the part that their marriage plays in the advancement of the Kingdom of God in the world.

Marriage isn't just two people learning to get along. It is a living demonstration of God's covenant with His creation. Every couple is an image bearer—a portrait of God's love for the world. If we are going to accurately reflect the image of God, we need to live our life together His way, with His mind.

Marriage Rx is a challenge to rise to a high calling. It is a vision of Christian marriage that goes from the root of love to the flower of destiny. It is a prescription for the healing of our relationship and an invitation to a radical marriage.

Acknowledgments

We owe a debt of gratitude to Jim and Marilyn who rose from ashes and took to the skies. They gave us hope for marriages everywhere.

We are grateful to the many friends who came to us with the gift of their need and then allowed us to join them in seeking the mind of the Father on their behalf.

We give our thanks to the men and women of Montavilla Baptist Church who eagerly received this material into their hearts and then offered their contribution to make it better.

God has given us marvelous comrades. We are grateful.

Chapter 1

Being "One Flesh"

Marriage Modeled by Trinity

> Jesus said, "The most important commandment is, 'Hear, O Israel: The Lord our God, the Lord is one. And you shall love the Lord your God with all your heart and with all your soul and with all your mind and with all your strength.' The second is this: 'You shall love your neighbor as yourself.' There is no other commandment greater than these." [1]

When asked about His priorities, Jesus did not hesitate to state them clearly: Love God. Love your neighbor. These are the most important. They apply to the most fundamental of relationships. When one of Jesus' listeners went so far as to ask what He meant by "neighbor," Jesus responded with one of the best known of all of His parables, the story of the Good Samaritan.

But the closest of all "neighbors" is not the unfortunate traveler who got mugged on the way to Jericho. Neither is he the person who lives in our town or on our street. The closest of all neighbors is the one we're married to, and if we are serious about keeping God's commandment to love our neighbor as ourselves, then we have to start there. The challenge is when you live close to someone day in and day out, you are reminded how different you really are from this "neighbor."

In the Marriage Rx seminar, we often use video clips to emphasize key aspects of the discussion. To illustrate the impact of personality differences in a marriage relationship we use a clip from the movie adaptation of Barefoot in the Park, a play by Neil Simon. In the scene, two young newlyweds, Paul and Corrie, are faced with the realization that they are really quite different from each other. Paul is the practical, rising-star attorney, straight-laced and dignified; Corrie is the free-spirited, idealistic adventuress. He is bewildered by his young wife's reckless abandon—she has been known to walk barefoot in the park in the middle of winter. She, on the other hand, has begun to see her new husband for the proper stick-in-the-mud that he really is—a stuffed shirt, incapable of having a good time!

Can such a mis-matched pair of lovers hope to survive each other's shortcomings? That is the theme of the film. Of course, in the end, love conquers all and they live happily ever after. And the audience leaves the theater comfortable in the assurance that Paul and Corrie will overcome whatever differences they have. They may even learn to love each other *because* they are different.

Is that what the Creator had in mind? In a word, yes.

Marriage is No Accident

Did you ever stop to consider this relationship we call marriage? The Bible is clear that it is God's idea. If we presume that God doesn't do things arbitrarily, then there must have been a reason. In other words, when it comes to marriage, it may be helpful to ask what I consider to be one of the most useful questions you can ask about matters of faith and life: Why?

So, why did God dream up this thing called marriage? What possible reason could He have had to require an institution that bound people together for life, even with all their differences? The question actually cuts even deeper. Why did He make two kinds of human beings—male and female—in the first place? He is God, after all. Couldn't He have made them more alike? Yes, He could have, but He didn't.

Why? Let us propose an answer: God made us male and female, that is sexual, so we would be able to understand Him.

Let me explain.

For starters, God is unique, one of a kind. He is the only one and there is no other. [2]

Here are a few things we know about Him:

First, He is three and also one. The theological code word for that concept is "Trinity." In scripture, there are three persons mentioned that are all called "God." But, there is only one God. So, how do you figure that one out? Let's attempt an illustration.

Let's start with the first few words of Genesis: "In the beginning, God created the heavens and the earth." OK, so in the beginning there was no heaven and no earth, there was just God. Then, He made heaven. Next He made earth.

Now, imagine a cardboard box—a fruit box. We'll call it heaven. And picture a shoe. Let's pretend that's earth. Finally, let's imagine you are God, standing next to the box and the shoe. You're bigger than both of them.

Slip your foot into the shoe (earth). Are you in "earth?" Yes, but not all of you. Only as much of you as this shoe-earth can contain.

Now, put your other foot into the box. Presto! You're in heaven...but not completely because it's too small to hold all of you. Even so, you're in the shoe and in the box. You are one person in two places at once. Not a perfect illustration, but it helps to understand how the one God might be more than one. Or, as it says in the Bible, how He can be "Father in heaven" and Jesus, "the Son of God and God the Son" in earth.

God created more than one dimension and then *expressed Himself* in each. That's how the Bible can say that Jesus Christ was responsible for creating the earth, as though He made it from the inside out! [3]

Describing a unique being like God has its challenges. Since we aren't able to fully comprehend His nature, the only way we can understand Him is by comparison. Without a frame of reference we have few other choices. We would have to do the same kind of thing if we had to describe the color red to a person who had been blind from birth. What is red? Well, it's a color that is like something hot or something loud like a siren. That's what red is like.

What is God like? If we didn't have some frame of reference or point of comparison He would be a complete mystery. But we do have a point of comparison: us. God created us in a way that made it possible for us to compare our world and our relationships to Him. The way the human race was created was purposeful, so we could imagine God. That's why the Bible says that the Creator made us in "His image."

What is God like? Like a father. Like a husband. We are like a child. Like a bride. We use the masculine pronoun when talking about God, not because He is male by nature, but because that imagery best describes Him. We are not sexual beings because sexuality defines who we are, but because it describes who God is. It is God's "prophetic creation"; a point of reference.

No wonder marriage is so important. The covenant relationship between a man and a woman communicates what God is like. Let's look at how that plays out in the Bible.

All in the Family

This kind of imagery appears throughout the Bible. Because God has created us male and female and designated a covenant relationship between them, He has a point of comparison that helps us envision our otherwise inscrutable God. In Isaiah, the prophet tells us that, "your Maker is your Husband."[4] In Jeremiah, the love of Israel for God is compared to the love of a bride.[5] In Ezekiel, God, in the role of the husband and redeemer, cares for his vulnerable bride.[6] Through the prophet, Hosea, God uses the imagery to describe the unfaithfulness of His people. In the entire book of Hosea, God is the husband to His people, regardless of their unfaithfulness to Him.

In Psalm 103, God becomes the compassionate father who cares for His children.[7] In Jeremiah and Malachi, He is identified as a Father to the Hebrew nation.[8] Even in the New Testament, God emerges as Father—Jesus taught His disciples to address God that way, and to live in that understanding. [9] Moreover, Jesus, Himself, is compared to a bridegroom and His followers to a bride. Koinonia, the Greek word that is most often used to mean "fellowship," has roots in the first century understanding of marriage.

It is from these metaphors that we get closer to being able to understand God, the unique, three-in-one Creator of the universe. Husbands and wives and the mystical bond of love that unites them are that triune image. Father, mother and children are a single family unit—a trinity. The husband, wife and God are a metaphor for the Father, Son and Holy Spirit.

Inasmuch as the comparison helps us understand the Creator, our marriage relationship then becomes a picture of God to others. God's prophetic creation of men and women and the covenant that binds them together is the image that communicates the nature of God to the watching world. No wonder the forces of evil work so hard to destroy and distort marriage. It is the very image of God's relationship with His creation.

As such, it is a tool in our hands to communicate God's love. This is why marriage becomes the relationship that makes the command to "love your neighbor as yourself" the most meaningful. Marriage, as a description of God and His people, becomes the very image of love—sacrificial and unbreakable. To the extent that we are faithful to live out those qualities, our marriage becomes a ministry to others and the means to better understand God as a husband and father to us.

Leave, Cleave and Weave

The Trinity is nearly incomprehensible to us—God the Father, a complete being that is merged with the Son and Spirit. The Son a separate person, yet merged with the Father and Spirit. The Spirit also distinct in Himself, yet made complete by the Father and Son. There is nothing in the natural world that adequately represents this distinctness and inseparable union, except the divine design of marriage.

There has to be trinity to demonstrate true love because it requires three parts. There is the lover, the one who prefers another over self. There is the loved, the one who is being preferred or the object of that love. Then there is the witness, the one who sees and appreciates the love.

The Trinity has always been, and the expression of love has always been. God the Father loves the Son, and the Holy Spirit admires that affection with approval. God the Son loves the Spirit, and the Father watches with delight. The Spirit loves the Father and the Son affirms it.

The expression and recognition of love is expressed as praise and glory. That glory is reflected by the Spirit as He witnesses the love. It is reflected by the Father likewise, and continues to expand through the Son. In the heavenly realm and throughout all creation the glory of God is magnified from one degree of glory to another.

> And we all, with unveiled face, beholding the glory of the Lord, are being transformed into the same image from one degree of glory to another. For this comes from the Lord who is the Spirit. [10]

That same union and glory is reflected through us since we are created in His image. The Apostle Paul writes that we begin to show it as we witness His glory. There is no more powerful way for that glory to be demonstrated on earth than through true love expressed in God's design for marriage.

Replication of the Trinity Pattern

The Pharisees in Judea came to test Jesus about His view on divorce, hoping to polarize Him among the crowd and discredit His ministry. Jesus responded to them with Scripture.

> He answered, "Have you not read that He who created them from the beginning made them male and female, and said, 'Therefore a man shall leave his father and his mother and hold fast to his wife, and the two shall become one flesh'? So they are no longer two but one flesh. What therefore God has joined together, let not man separate." [11]

He goes on to explain that the union between a husband and wife is not like an earthly compound that can be separated into its individual parts, but is a heavenly representation of the Trinity. When we understand these principles it gives us insight to how we are designed. We can live by these principles to be in compliance with that design. Things go better when we work like we were designed to work.

Within this verse we see the replication of the Trinity. It says "a man shall leave his father and mother...." There are three individuals in the Trinity: Father, Son and Holy Spirit. Notice the three persons in this verse: man, father and mother. Each person has a role to play in the union.

Watch as the pattern develops. The man leaves the father and mother just like Jesus as the Son had to leave the Father and Spirit to come to earth as a man. Leaving requires separation, and Jesus became separated from the Father and Spirit. The distinctions between the persons of the Trinity are emphasized in this process.

The purpose of the separation is so the man can be joined to his wife. Jesus was separated from heaven to be joined to His wife, the church. The step of distinction opens the way for a new union to be formed. The verse describes this union by saying: "and shall hold fast to his wife."

Notice the replication of the Trinity and pick out the three persons. There is a husband and a wife holding fast together as a new entity, with God as the witness. Three distinct pieces, yet one new Trinity. As the husband loves his wife, God watches on as witness. As God loves the wife, the husband acts as witness, and as the husband loves God, the wife is witness. Glory expands, from glory to glory.

The new entity gets a new name. In most marriage ceremonies there comes a moment when the minister announces the completion of the union to the audience by saying: "I now present to you Mr. and Mrs. Surname." They are no longer two, but joined together in a supernatural union. A Christian marriage reflects the Trinity in this way.

The Scripture goes on to say: "and the two shall become one flesh." Not only are they joined together, but they are welded together. Their personalities merge and the distinctions become less and less. They are joined physically, emotionally and spiritually. They seem inseparable, though never because one absorbs the other. This is the picture we have of God as the Trinity.

One expression of love is the deep desire to know and to be known. This reflects the omniscient character of God. It becomes an intimacy that leads to oneness and breaks down barriers between the personalities. It helps define the new creation.

This intimacy also leads to fruitfulness. As we have seen before, God's glory and love is always expanding, leading to creation. We are created in His image. That is why He commands us to be fruitful and multiply. The expression of love, combined with the divine spark of creation, creates a child. It is how we replicate the Trinity pattern: one flesh plus creation. Notice the three persons: father and mother (one flesh) plus child (creation).

The replication of the Trinity in a marriage is also like Christ and the church. A nonbeliever becomes a new entity by becoming identified with Christ, much like a bride becomes identified with her husband. Jesus is like the man that leaves father and mother to be joined to his wife, the church. Paul declares the mysterious nature of this union.

> This mystery is profound, and I am saying that it refers to Christ and the church. [12]

Just as a husband and wife become a new entity, Christ and the believer also receive a new surname: Christian. Christ is not just a man, however. He is also a spirit. For that reason, the union is complete as they become both one flesh and one spirit.

> But he who is joined to the Lord becomes one spirit with Him. [13]

The outcome is for Christian marriages to be an accurate representation of the true love demonstrated by Christ for the church. There is true love and respect displayed between husband and wife, just as proclaimed by the Apostle Paul:

> However, let each one of you love his wife as himself, and let the wife see that she respects her husband. [14]

True love and respect are expressed and reflected between husband and wife. This is witnessed by God and brings praise. It builds from glory to glory because each expression reflects God's character, bringing Him glory. It is reflected through each of us, as we are merged with Him. Then it is witnessed by others, bringing glory to God. As it is witnessed by our children, the replication of the Trinity is prepared for another generation.

> Therefore a man shall leave his father and his mother and hold fast to his wife, and they shall become one flesh. [15]

Let us take a practical look at these steps outlined in Genesis 2:24 since they so clearly describe the process God had in mind for marriage.

Leave

Perhaps you have never thought about this first step in the marriage process, but you have to move away from the past in order to establish the future. The man must leave his old life, his old way of living, even his old identity so he can build a new oneness with his wife.

As we discussed earlier, you must leave father and mother to replicate the Trinity pattern. Since it is God's design for marriage that we are after, it makes sense to do it His way.

You must leave the past to gain the potential to create that new and separate identity. This is the process of regeneration. Incomplete leaving puts the person in bondage to the old identity instead of making them free to establish something new.

For example, when we (Calvin and Julie) were first married we lived in a small college town in Iowa, about a two hour drive from Julie's parents. We enjoyed visiting them on weekends, from time to time...especially when we needed some good food and warm hospitality.

On the way home one Sunday evening, I very carefully broached a sensitive subject: "Honey, when we are visiting your folks, you change. It's like you're a different person around them." I said. "And I don't really like that person as much as I normally like you."

This sparked some lively discussion as we worked through the various responses to that observation. The "conversation ball" was passed back and forth in some impressive volleys. I would say we have learned a lot about healthy ways to communicate since those early days.

"What do you mean, 'I'm different?'" she asked.

"It's like you regress. You act like a little girl again, especially around your mom. Instead of the confidence you usually have, you ask them what you should do. Instead of talking with me about things, you listen to them and I don't know what my role is. It's just different than when we're by ourselves."

Our discussion went in a positive direction as we explored this phenomenon. She could see how the old role of being a daughter influenced her behavior, and how easily she reverted to it. She had not intended to, but it was familiar and comfortable, especially in that setting. She needed to leave her home emotionally as well as physically so her new identity, Mrs. Julie Tadema, could develop.

You must also leave your father and mother in order to establish appropriate authority and control in the relationship. Ultimate authority belongs to God and then to the household through the husband and wife. We will cover this in greater detail in a later chapter. Unless you leave your parents' household there is confusion over authority and responsibility. Leaving helps define the areas of influence and allows the couple to work out their obedience to the Lord.

During that first year of marriage, we became too familiar with the adjustment struggles of the young couple living above our apartment. During the week we heard their conversational volleys, most frequently punctuated with a sudden communication break. The young wife would inevitably leave the apartment to go to her parents' home, just fifteen miles away. This often happened on Friday just as classes were over.

The young woman would go home for some encouragement and perhaps to marshal some support for her position. She would pour out her heart to her mom. Unfortunately, her mother was giving her that support by agreeing with her, saying: "You poor baby; he's a wretch." Of course, this was not helping the couple establish their own relationship.

This is not an uncommon scenario. In this example the young lady did a poor job of leaving her father and mother so she could be joined to her husband. At the same time, her parents did a poor job of encouraging her to leave.

What does leaving look like physically?

There are cultural and traditional aspects to consider as you work out the answer to this question. Also, it does not mean you must break those relationships, but that they must be allowed to change.

In most cases it means to move out from under the roof of the parents, becoming independent for such things as food and shelter. As a rule of thumb, the proximity should be in inverse proportion to the force that would hold you back into the old identity. Physical separation enhances the couple's problem solving skills and reliance on each other, and includes the proper use of barriers and limits.

What does leaving look like emotionally?

It is a pronounced shift of emotional ties from parents and family to your spouse. This does not exclude emotional relationship with your parents, but changes the frame of reference for your emotional health. It shifts the source of your emotional grounding.

For example, the primary source for affirmation of your identity and character now comes from your spouse instead of your parents. The same is true for your source of comfort or encouragement. Leaving your parents emotionally creates a void that can be filled by emotional development as a couple.

What does leaving look like spiritually?

God's plan for family living is that the father be the spiritual leader of the household. Replicating the Trinity requires the spiritual leadership mantle to be passed. The husband leaves his father's spiritual covering and takes on that role for his own home. The wife leaves her father's spiritual covering to accept her husband in that role.

There are other spiritual ties in a family that must be reassigned, especially in the way spiritual gifts are mixed and blended. As a couple becomes unified, they bring a different gift mix to the body of Christ. This can only happen when the old relationships are given a chance to change.

Cleave

It is an old fashioned word that means to be joined together, to adhere, or to hold fast. We use this word because some people are familiar with it in this context from the King James Version of the Bible. We also use it because it rhymes.

The purpose of leaving is so that the two individuals can be joined together to create something new. It is analogous to two atoms that combine together in a chemical reaction to form a new compound. Individually they have characteristics distinct to their elemental properties, but together they have the new properties of a compound.

Remember that this joining together is a replication of the Trinity pattern. Just as God the Father, God the Son, and God the Holy Spirit are separate Persons, they are joined as one God. They are simultaneously separate and merged. It is that kind of joining that describes the husband and wife union. They are simultaneously separate and merged.

Two individuals come together to discover how they complement one another and fit together as a new entity. A solid union happens because of differences, and it is true that opposites attract. Uniformity works against this kind of cleaving. Like interlocking pieces to a jigsaw puzzle, your strengths and weaknesses are balanced between you.

When you first come together, you will not fit. You learn to fit together by loving one another. Paul gives us good instruction on this point:

> Complete my joy by being of the same mind, having the same love, being in full accord and of one mind. Do nothing from rivalry or conceit, but in humility count others more significant than yourselves. Let each of you look not only to his own interests, but also the interests of others. [16]

Paraphrased for a couple, it would say "to be in full accord and one mind (cleave) look not to your own interests but to the interests of your spouse as well." You adapt to each other by exercising this kind of selfless love. In every interaction, including conflict, you give preference to your spouse.

My wife, Julie, grew up in a middle class home with one sister and never shared a bedroom with anyone until she went away to college. Less than two years later we were married and she was suddenly sharing everything, a room and even a bed. As great as that is, it still takes adjustment when it has not been your experience. It is a new way of living.

You must interact together, even facing conflict, to build a healthy authority and control system. The Trinity model of marriage is equal personhood under God's authority. This is tested and proven through healthy management of challenges, and then becomes strong enough to depend on even under the most stressful circumstances.

Joining, adjusting, and discovering how you fit together begins with simple things like sharing a bedroom. It grows so you can handle increasingly difficult situations, such as raising children or dealing with financial or health stress. God has a way of allowing challenges that will strengthen your relationship, so you can take advantage of adapting to one another in love.

What does cleaving look like physically?

At a very practical level this looks like moving into the same house or apartment together. Sexual intimacy is a physical representation of joining, but cleaving goes beyond this. It also means sharing a bedroom, kitchen, storage closet and garage. It is to join your stuff in a combination of personal and communal things. For example, clothing is a personal thing while laundry is communal, even though they are comprised of the same articles.

Cleaving in the physical realm also looks like joining in some of the more routine things, such as budget, chores and roles. You have a new perception of these things as a couple because they are defined by your interaction and connectedness in that area.

What does cleaving look like emotionally?

Emotional cleaving means to learn to depend on each other instead of your family of origin or others. It means processing emotional responses together, not running home to your family, or to your girlfriend's, or to your co-workers, or the stranger at the bar or coffee shop.

Joining together in an emotional response to situations or beliefs demonstrates sympathy with each other. The word "empathy" is used to describe one person knowing how another feels, and this is an individual application of emotional response. Sympathy means that your emotions are synchronized, which is the result of being joined.

Cleaving emotionally is also demonstrated in preparation for a circumstance or situation, and not just in response to it. Joy and peace are examples of shared emotions that can be made stronger by reflecting between the husband and wife. It is not accurate to say they share responsibility for emotions, but they share the result of them together.

What does cleaving look like spiritually?

Coming together spiritually happens when you begin to practice spiritual disciplines together. That means having devotions or reading the Bible together. It also means praying together. Not just in the traditional way of asking God to 'bless this food," but truly seeking His heart on a matter and together listening for His response.

Weave

Following the pattern of leave and cleave, we use the word "weave" to represent the union of husband and wife into one flesh. It suggests the intertwining of thread to make a piece of fabric, perhaps even in a pattern or picture. You have to look very closely to distinguish the individual threads, but the full effect comes from seeing it as a whole.

The marriage relationship is built upon complete intimacy. The promise is that "the two shall become one flesh." God has designed it so the relationship merges two separate identities until they are enmeshed at the cellular level. It is not just being joined, like two people hanging together, but co-joined inseparably.

This is the mystery that is a replication of the Trinity pattern. We see it proclaimed prophetically in these verses:

> Two are better than one, because they have a good reward for their toil. For if they fall, one will lift up his fellow. But woe to him who is alone when he falls and has not another to lift him up! Again, if two lie together, they keep warm, but how can one keep warm alone? And though a man might prevail against one who is alone, two will withstand him--a threefold cord is not quickly broken. [17]

Notice the development in this passage that represents the weaving. Two are better than one, and then proof is given. Two are better at keeping each other warm. Two are better at defending against attack. Then suddenly the picture changes: a threefold cord. The metaphors apply to the marriage relationship: two, two, two, and three. The last depiction is the completed symbolism of the Trinity pattern: husband plus wife plus God woven together as a single unit.

· A husband and wife enter togetherness by forging a new and single identity. They are no longer two pieces or separate identities, but merge into one. This is both described and promised by God in Genesis 2:24.

God's design uses sexual intimacy to create a "soul tie" which binds a husband and wife together. It is part of God's promise that sexual union will make two into one person, so that they become one flesh. This great gift is a spiritual transaction, meaning that it occurs at a level beyond what we perceive on earth. This is the reason that Jesus exclaimed:

"Let not man separate" as recorded in Matthew 19 and Mark 10.

This is a great gift for a husband and wife, and is the benefit that God intended. We will discuss the problems associated with soul ties due to infidelity or promiscuity in a later chapter. The same unifying property that bonds a husband and wife together is inappropriately applied between non-spousal relationships and must be broken.

To properly understand this weaving concept requires the use of new math. You may be familiar with the basics of arithmetic, and firmly avow that one plus one equals two. The new math requires multiplication: one times one equals one. This is the description of the Trinity pattern in a marriage.

What does weaving look like physically?

Sex. More specifically, sexual intimacy. It is the physical union of two bodies as close to becoming one flesh as is physically possible. This is not the sex act because that is just a physical activity for self-gratification. In the "Me" generation it represented free love, by which people meant they were free to love themselves. In the "Hookup" generation it represents freedom to engage in casual sex, by which people mean they are free to care less about their partner. Nor is it the physical tool for conquest or control that robs the identity of one for the sake of the other. This is the physical union prescribed by God as the means to know and be known. God blesses this union with a soul tie.

It is small wonder that this act of weaving should be the active ingredient in having children. Being a family is what weaving looks like physically. Children combine the heredity and environment of their parents in a replication process. The father and mother become inextricably woven together through the common needs of this family.

What does weaving look like emotionally?

We mentioned in the section above that empathy (knowing how another feels) and sympathy (feeling what another feels) are consistent with emotional cleaving. A husband and wife that are woven together emotionally will know what the other feels and will feel the same way, for the same reason. Their emotional response to any given situation will not only be synchronized, but shared. Although, in most cases they will express the emotion differently.

Any trial or conflict presents an opportunity for you to establish priorities of your core values. As a couple merges their core values into one, they will experience this oneness in emotional responses. The weaving process can take some time, but it always has a goal in mind: oneness.

What does weaving look like spiritually?

Weaving has everything to do with identity rather than behavior. You will share a single spiritual identity with your spouse as the weaving is completed. Your identities will have merged together just as they are one with God. Jesus proclaimed this in His High Priestly prayer:

> The glory that You have given Me I have given to them, that they may be one even as We are one, I in them and You in me, that they may become perfectly one, so that the world may know that You sent Me and loved them even as You loved Me. [18]

This description of love and oneness is complete compatibility and inseparable identities. As the Trinity pattern requires, the separate persons are merged into a single identity with God as the standard of truth. Then it will be said of you:

> "For who has understood the mind of the Lord so as to instruct him?" But we have the mind of Christ. [19]

Committed to Each Other

When we are working with a couple that comes for encouragement, one of the first questions we will ask of each is how committed they are to making their marriage work. The answer they give speaks volumes about where they have been and where they are likely to go.

How committed are you to making this work?

Undoubtedly you know the "right" answer: "I'm 100% committed. I'm all in. Everything is on the table. I'll do anything it takes to get this right." We call this the Sunday School answer, because it is so obviously the right answer that people will say it even if they don't really know what it means.

The phrase "all in" comes from the rules of poker, the card game about winning something of value (money) from others. The rules require fair and orderly betting so the pot is even and all the players have equal chance to win. If a player is unable to match an opponent's bet they can still call the pot by declaring "all in." In essence, it means that they are putting all of their available resources on the line for this hand. Win or lose, their future in the game depends on the outcome of this hand. Everything is at stake.

If you aren't one flesh, and if you aren't all in, the best you can hope for in your marriage is compromise. The kingdom of the world assumes limited resources that must be divided among the people, and it makes that exchange based on control, greed and fear. A marriage of compromise will never reach a satisfactory conclusion, for either party, because it concerns itself with what is lacking.

God's way of replicating the Trinity pattern creates something new. The heavenly kingdom assumes a benevolent Creator that gives and receives, being fruitful and multiplying in all areas. A one-flesh marriage is that new identity, created in the image of God and able to participate in the heavenly kingdom.

0 % Committed

One possible answer to the question of commitment is "zero percent." In other words, this person is not at all committed to making the marriage work. Before marriage this is indicated by the worldly question: "Are we going to be compatible? Will you fit with me?" After marriage some still ask these questions as a condition for commitment. It won't work if one or both of the partners are zero percent committed. It may be an honest answer, but there is no extra credit for honesty in this sense when it comes to working on a marriage.

You may be wondering if people ever say they are zero percent committed. The answer is yes. It is borne out of selfishness, and indicates that the person is somewhere in the continuum between self-aware, self-centered and narcissistic (a personality disorder). It is also a sign of immaturity, demonstrating that the person has not grown past the infant / child stage of learning to relate with others in their world.

One man confessed this to me with surprising candor. He was willing to have a great marriage if that was how it worked out, but he wasn't willing to work at it. I challenged him about his passive response by asking him if he knew what he should do. Yes, he knew what God commanded him to do, the ethical and moral thing to do, and the pragmatic thing for the sake of their children. Despite all that, he chose not to engage. He was not committed.

There is no hope that this marriage will replicate the Trinity pattern. The projected outcome is for them to separate physically, as they have emotionally and spiritually. They could coexist in parallel lives, held in dynamic tension with strong boundaries and limits, but the conflict between them will show up as pain. It is not a pretty picture. It is certainly not a depiction of God's character.

50% Committed

Another answer to the question of commitment is: "I'm totally committed to this marriage, and will share myself with you equally." It comes across as being fair. The person feels they are giving as much to the other as they are keeping for themselves, half for each.

I call this the fifty-percent commitment. Though it sounds magnanimous, it really means the person will withhold at least half of their identity from the partnership. The result of this kind of marriage is compromise. It leads to comparison and judgment. It puts a positive spin on the term "give and take" but does not fairly represent the picture of God: give and receive.

One of the symptoms of this kind of marriage is the use of separate scorecards. He keeps track of what he gives in exchange for what he expects to take in return. She keeps track from her perspective in a form of check and balance. Problems arise because of "differing measures," which God detests according to the Bible. His evaluation does not match hers because there isn't a common standard.

The result of a life of compromise and division is that each must work twice as hard to keep what they want, and it always ends in regrets. For instance, he wants a new car, so in fairness they buy one for each. She chooses one vacation destination and he the next, but to be totally fair they are satisfied only half the time. The dissatisfaction leads to escalation of demands. Soon the giving can not keep pace and regrets turn into suspicion and then blame.

The fifty percent committed answer will not lead to marital happiness. Though it sounds fair and equal, it is a divide and separate strategy that breaks down over time. The one plus one equals two formula does not add up to a team. If you keep scorecards, or even a mental checklist, reconsider your commitment level to see if you are answering the question this way.

100% Committed to Me

Another answer we hear is: "I'm all in, one hundred percent committed, because this marriage has to work." When we dig a little deeper we discover that he or she should have said: "I'm one hundred percent committed to me." They are willing to do anything they can to make things work out, because it is in their own best interest.

You can see this attitude displayed in greeting cards, romantic comedies, novels, and other depictions of modern romance. Consider phrases such as: "I like me best when I'm with you" or "You complete me." While it sounds like love, it is far removed from sacrificial love. Its foundation is a selfish desire.

You may see similarities between this commitment level and what is described above as zero percent committed. They are two sides of the same coin. This selfishness is expressed proactively instead of passively. It is the selfish expression of the aggressive personality compared to the passive one. Abusive relationships are likely to fall in this category.

One man with this commitment told me, "I thought life was like a movie about me, and my wife and family are the supporting cast. The movie can't be made without them." Of course, he meant that the movie couldn't be made without someone in that role, but in fact anyone could fill the role.

The best a marriage can hope for with this commitment level is that the husband and wife leave their father and mother and cleave together. They are able to join, but not become one flesh. They will cohabitate and live parallel lives as long as it is mutually beneficial. In practice we see that whenever the parallel lives cross they experience conflict instead of union. The reason is that the model is set up to preserve self.

100% Committed to You

Sometimes we hear people say: "I'm all in, one-hundred percent committed, because this marriage has to work" when what they should say is "I'm one-hundred percent committed to you." They are willing to give anything to make things work out, because they are devoted to the best interests of the other.

You see this attitude displayed in greeting cards, romantic songs, comedies and novels, just like the one above. "I'm wholly devoted to you" is an example, or "I'd give all I have…" While it sounds like love, it is far removed from mutuality and being one flesh.

This is an example of being unequally yoked. One person is willing to pay anything for the other's happiness, comfort, or expectations. In so doing, they become the victim in the relationship. They will experience loss of self as the other absorbs it. Loss of voice, loss of dreams, loss of vision are the main ways their personality takes a back seat to the other. When these things are not expressed in a healthy way, the person is unable to develop to their full identity in Christ.

A marriage that is built on one or both partners being one hundred percent committed to the other will be two people living parallel lives. The difference between this and the example above, is that the committed person's identity is absorbed by the other instead of merged with it.

We often see a marriage built on both of these answers, each person is all in but for opposite reasons. It ends up being a one-sided partnership and has all the ingredients for abuse. Unfortunately, a person may seek out this kind of relationship because they believe this is what love looks like.

100% Committed to Us

Of course, this is the right answer. When a husband is totally committed to his wife through the marriage, and she is totally committed to her husband through the marriage the trinity model is replicated. Each is able to leave their former self and become merged into a new creation. The husband and wife become a new identity that exists because they are together.

In this act of creation, there must be a dying and regeneration. The dying to "self" that is described in the Bible means the old nature of individualism is put to death. Once it is dead, then the new identity can be resurrected. It looks different because it is different.

When a husband dies to himself, God raises up his identity in Christ and regenerates a merged identity with his wife. When the wife dies to herself, God raises up her identity in Christ and she is able to merge as well. Instead of give and take, this relationship is built on give and receive.

> He answered, "Have you not read that he who created them from the beginning made them male and female, and said, 'Therefore a man shall leave his father and his mother and hold fast to his wife, and the two shall become one flesh'? So they are no longer two but one flesh. What therefore God has joined together, let not man separate." [20]

God does the creative work, and they are no longer two but one flesh.

Mature in Unity

> I do not ask on behalf of these alone, but for those also who believe in Me through their word, that they may all be one; even as You, Father, are in Me and I in You, that they also may be in Us, so

that the world may believe that You sent Me. The glory which You have given Me I have given to them, that they may be one, just as We are one, I in them and You in Me, that they may be perfected in unity, so that the world may know that You sent Me, and loved them, even as You have loved Me.[21]

In the above verses, Jesus was praying for His disciples. The scene is what we call "The Last Supper," the time that Jesus had set aside to be with His disciples before His arrest and eventual execution. This was a critical time, made all the more important because in just a few hours He was to be taken from them. There were loose ends to be tied up—unfinished business—so what Jesus had to say to His Father about the disciples invites our careful notice. More so, because He is praying that the disciples will have an impact on the world. He is praying that they will do what is necessary in order to have world-changing influence.

So, what did He pray? That they, the disciples (and all that came to an understanding of the gospel through them) would be one. The way He put it: that they may be *perfected in unity*. At first glance, He seems to be praying that the disciples will get really good at being unified—get along well. Taken this way, it suggests that the goal of the church is to attain unity.

But, can we understand the Lord's request differently? What if we take Him to mean that we will become mature (because that's what the word, "perfect" means) as we live in a condition of unity; that living together in unity is the means by which we will *become* perfect.

Consider an illustration.

Let's say you're going to bake a cake. You have all the ingredients gathered; all the equipment—cups, spoons and all that. You mix everything together in their proper proportions and pour the mixture into a pan. Are you done? No. One important thing remains before you're ready to serve your cake. It needs to be baked. All those ingredients will not be a cake fit to serve until they have been thoroughly mixed, placed in the oven and heated. Only that will bring this cooking project to completion. The cake isn't about the heat of the oven, but the heat of the oven makes the cake ready for its purpose: to serve your family or your guests.

We can understand Jesus' prayer in a similar way. Jesus is praying that God's covenant gift of unity will serve the purpose for which it was intended: to grow us up; make us mature. The goal of Jesus' prayer isn't unity; it is maturity. Unity is the oven—the environment—that heats people (a church, a group, even a couple) to make them ready to serve.

The apostle Paul spoke often about unity. To him, unity had to do with treating others with respect and honor; moreover' he told his students in the faith that each should treat the other as though he were more important than himself. [22] When Paul wrote to the church in Ephesus, he said,

> ...live worthily of the calling with which you have
> been called, with all humility and gentleness, with
> patience, bearing with one another in love,
> making every effort to keep the unity of the Spirit
> in the bond of peace." [23]

When we understand unity—or "oneness"—to be the means by which each of us grows more mature, we can understand Paul (not to mention, Jesus!) and his passion to see disciples love one another.

And why is growing together toward maturity so important? Because there is a fallen world in need of rescue and restoration. Our covenant commitment to live in oneness is "basic training" for the larger goal of advancing the Kingdom in the world. That training happens wherever independence yields to the higher value of interdependence; in a community of hundreds or a marriage of two.

But, here's the challenge of unity: oneness is not "sameness." Being unified is not being uniform. Instead, the oneness that brings maturity means to love one another beyond and through our differences—what Jesus called being "perfected in unity." It means seeing the whole community as being greater than its parts and recognizing the implications of that; we are called to regard others without reference to our own need. That is the backbone of a godly marriage, something called "covenant," a topic we will talk about in more detail in Chapter Two. This covenant concept was the way the human race was to interact from the very beginning, a relational rhythm that got lost in the garden. To find it again will require us to practice oneness in our day-to-day life; in the way we see our marriage, family and community; even in the way we talk to each other.

New Pronouns

Remember that this unity, or weaving, makes the two become one flesh; it is something entirely new. Just as this requires new math (not one plus one equals two, but one times one equals one) it also requires new language. The new identity needs a new name, and in conversation this will be demonstrated by the use of new pronouns. You will not use "I, me, my, you, or your" but instead "us, we, and our."

Aside from the kiss, the most meaningful moment of the wedding ceremony is when the couple is introduced for the first time as "Mr. and Mrs. Surname." A change of name is appropriate with the change of identity.

In the Bible we see significant name changes. Abram becomes Abraham. Jacob becomes Israel. Simon becomes Peter. Saul becomes Paul. You understand from prophecy that everyone will have a new name in heaven. The name change accompanies a significant spiritual transaction.

In the legal world we see the same consideration given to the creation of a new identity. A birth certificate legally names the one born, and this is the beginning of the association of name and person. A corporation is assigned a name upon creation, and that name is assigned to it as long as the corporate entity exists. A merger between corporations and a merger between personal identities are also signified by a new name.

Whether on heaven or earth, newness of life is represented by a name change.

Your conversations should reflect this name change as you agree with the newness of your marriage identity. Pronouns are the words we use in place of names, so listen to your conversation to see how completely you have embraced the new name concept. 'I', 'me' and 'my' are the old names you use for yourself. 'You' and 'your' are the old names you use for your spouse. See how often you slip into the old names instead of using the new name (us, we and our).

This is more than just an exercise in linguistics. Words have meanings, and what you say comes from your heart. Examining your words is more effective than an X-ray or MRI for knowing your internal condition.

Is your conversation spiked with "you" and "your?" These names indicate accusation and blame. Their use verbally separates your spouse's identity from your own, making distinctions between feelings, motives and respon-sibilities. Perhaps you can easily imagine the nonverbal message that goes along with the use of "you" and "your" in conversation: a finger pointing at the other person for emphasis. This physical reminder punctuates the gap bet-ween two people in a way that encourages increased distance.

Is your conversation spiked with "I" and "me" and "my?" These names indicate "self" as in self-defense and self-interest. They communicate protectionism as they also create verbal separation between your spouse's identity and your own. Perhaps you can easily imagine the nonverbal message that goes along with the use of the first person pronouns: a finger (or thumb) pointing to yourself for emphasis. This physical reminder also punctuates the gap between two people, but does so in the opposite direction.

Instead, you should be in the habit of using the plural first person pronouns such as "us" and "we" and "our." These pronouns indicate sharing, joining, helping, teaming up, and strengthening. The message is punctuated with a feeling of union and a subtle reminder of being a new creation. Listen to the difference in these examples:

"Your children caused quite a ruckus at the picnic." This is likely to be followed with the question: "What are you going to do about it?" Notice the blaming and then a shift of responsibility.

"Our children caused quite a ruckus at the picnic." This is likely to be followed with the question: "What are we going to do about it?" Notice the mutual acceptance of blame, and more importantly the acknowledgement of mutual responsibility.

You can see by this example that a new way of talking brings about a new way of thinking. Consider this example from the apostle Paul:

> For the wife does not have authority over her own body, but the husband does. Likewise the husband does not have authority over his own body, but the wife does. Do not deprive one another, except perhaps by agreement for a limited time, that you may devote yourselves to prayer; but then come together again, so that Satan may not tempt you because of your lack of self-control. [24]

The concept of intimacy is a unique biblical expression of oneness meaning "all" and "everything." It is not understood by the world because it was born in the spiritual realm. Here we see that the wife and husband each give up their individual rights to physical bodies for the sake of each other, and merge their prayer life in the same way. Depriving one another can only happen when rights are separated and individuals are operating separately instead of as a union.

All you have, and all you are, is merged to form the new identity. When you catch yourself using the old pronouns (I, me and my) you will discover what you are withholding from one another. If it is "my" thing, then I'm withholding it from "us." When you catch yourself using the old pronouns (you and your) you will discover what you are rejecting from one another. If it is "your" thing, then I'm unwilling to make it part of "us."

It would be great if couples would learn the secret of new language when they are newlyweds. As they are merging their pasts, which are by definition separate, they would discover quickly what they are accepting and rejecting. For instance, the husband that refers to "your student loans" would see a place that his heart has not accepted part of his wife. Alternatively, his reference to "my golfing vacation" would see a place that his heart has not invited his wife.

It is interesting that the word "cleave" in the English language can mean both joining together and separating. We have used it in the context of being joined together, and talked about how commitment and conversation can enhance this joining. Conflict can also be used to test and prove the new identity.

Conflict acts as a wedge between separable selves. A mineralogist will cleave a crystal by separating one piece from another along a particular line determined by the chemical structure. This is how they create facets on a diamond.

When a husband and wife view themselves as "I and me" versus "you", it creates a condition in which separation can happen. Conflict acts as a wedge to force that separation along that line. In spiritual warfare these vulnerabilities are attacked through temptation and sin, designed to drive you apart. One of the enemy's primary goals is to destroy unions that represent the nature of God.

Conflict can also act as a weld between inseparable selves. The couple that lives according to the new identity, using pronouns like "we" and "us" and "our," is inseparable. They will face the conflict together and form a stronger bond as they fight as one against the opposition. Any event or attack will bring out better responses according to the perspectives, gifts, abilities and experiences each brings to the union. Together, in the Trinity pattern, best thinking will happen and the unit becomes stronger.

Use conflict to weld yourselves together. Watch your use of pronouns to indicate if you are being tempted to oppose each other instead of the opposition.

Walking by the Spirit

Comedienne Rita Rudner said, "I love being married. It's so great to find that one special person you want to annoy for the rest of your life." The reason her statement is part of a comedy routine is that nobody gets married hoping that in a few months or years they can both make each other miserable! On the contrary, we get married because we desire love, stability and companionship. But as we continue to explore the concept of being one flesh together, we need to remind ourselves that there is yet another reason, a more important one.

While we were preparing the Marriage Rx material the Tademas and the Mayhews spent considerable time together planning. On the evening before the first prototype gathering, as we began to pray over the direction of the teaching, I (Jody) was startled as I closed my eyes to hear what I am confident was a word from the Lord. He said, "This is not about *your* marriages, it is about *mine*."

His marriage? What could that mean?

In the letter of the Apostle Paul to the church in Ephesus, we get the answer. As Paul encouraged the followers there, he told the church that they should live, "submitting to one another out of reverence for Christ." Then he described how that should be practiced by wives and husbands. Here is what he said:

> Wives, submit to your own husbands, as to the Lord. For the husband is the head of the wife even as Christ is the head of the church, his body, and is himself its Savior. Now as the church submits to Christ, so also wives should submit in everything to their husbands. Husbands, love your wives, as Christ loved the church and gave himself up for her, that he might sanctify her, having cleansed her by the washing of water with the word, so that he might present the church to himself in splendor, without spot or wrinkle or any such thing, that she might be holy and without blemish. In the same way husbands should love their wives as their own bodies. He who loves his wife loves himself. For no one ever hated his own flesh, but nourishes and cherishes it, just as Christ does the church, because we are members of his body. "Therefore a man shall leave his father and mother and hold fast to his wife, and the two shall become one flesh." This mystery is profound, and I am saying that it refers to Christ and the church. [25]

As we wrote earlier, gender relationships are part of God's "prophetic creation" revealing to the human race clues to God's personality and character. Nowhere is that more revealing than in the relationship—covenant relationship—we call marriage. It is in that union that we are to demonstrate the oneness of God's character and allow that union to inform our relationship as husbands and wives. Indeed, it is that unity in relationship that brings us to maturity, as baking produces a finished cake.

Unfortunately, that doesn't come easy to us. It would be easier if we had a good pattern to follow, an example to observe and put into practice, but many of us lack that example. My family life (Jody) while growing up was pretty dysfunctional. It offered few clues to what oneness looked like. My upbringing was sadly lacking in any role model of oneness. More frequently I observed division. So, in order to learn to operate in unity and oneness, both Dan and I had to look beyond our family experiences and toward examples in scripture.

This process is what is often called "learning to walk in the Spirit." It begins with the condition of being born again and the concurrent awakening to the work of the Holy Spirit in our lives. Of course, when that happens we don't instantly step into maturity. That takes time. Though we may have become a new creation, there are lots of old habits that, for most of us, die hard.

Let's take a look at how old patterns die and new life takes hold in our hearts. To do that we need to consider how God created human beings.

First, He created us with a body. The human body is a beautiful, complex and fantastic thing, don't you agree? All of its systems and capabilities are nothing short of amazing. Second, he endowed every human with a soul, traditionally the seat of our mind, will and emotions. That is the part of our makeup that is tasked with helping us navigate this physical realm in which we live. The soul is the software, if you will, that helps us make sense of the world our body must interact with.

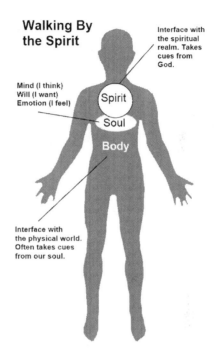

Walking By the Spirit

Interface with the spiritual realm. Takes cues from God.

Mind (I think)
Will (I want)
Emotion (I feel)

Spirit

Soul

Body

Interface with the physical world. Often takes cues from our soul.

But the fundamental part of our being is not body or soul, it is spirit. Remember, we were created in the image of God, and God is Spirit. The human creature as designed had a body, had a soul, but each human creature *was, and is*, spirit. And it was that component, the spiritual one, which, in the beginning, had the capacity to interact with God and the realm of the spiritual. In that pristine condition, our first parents had the ability to walk with their Creator in oneness, and therefore they were able to walk together in unity as they interacted with the world around them. When the human race was spiritually alive it had a great capacity for oneness

That was then. What about now?

Now, things are different because of the event called "the fall," that incident when humans made the decision to function outside of oneness with their Creator, even though they could have continued in unbroken relationship. The result of that rebellion caused a devastating change in the structure of the human personality. The spiritual sense that was part of the original design ceased to function. There had been a direct line to the spiritual realm, but the act of disobedience in the garden cut that link as sure as a hurricane blows down the cell tower upon which we depend for communication.

Of course that didn't mean that Adam and Eve immediately dropped dead. They remained alive, but with a critical difference. Whereas, they once had navigated their world with input from their spirit and its direct link with their Creator, now that linkage was no longer available. They were free of the connection with God—terrifyingly free. Just imagine the diagram above without the "spirit" part. What is left? The soul is left to navigate independently. Rather than take its cues from God, the human mind, will and emotions began to make its decisions based on its own conclusions and take its cues from the physical world.

And that's the way it has been ever since. It is as though the CEO of our lives isn't available and corporate operations are being handled by mid-management.

We are all familiar with this condition. Unless we come to a relationship with God, we make our decisions by the strength of our soul—I think it. I feel it. I want it. That kind of living comes naturally to us because the "spirit interface" is inoperable. We have no other source of input. That is what is so life-changing about being born again—getting saved. The spirit becomes alive again because of Jesus Christ.

Dan and I used to have an old radio. It didn't work, but it had a beautiful wooden cabinet and served as a piece of furniture in our living room. We put pictures on it, or an occasional vase filled with flowers. I can't imagine how we would have reacted if suddenly, as we went about our daily routine, that old radio had crackled to life and began to work as it had been originally designed.

That's kind of what happens when our spirit is revived at salvation. It switches on and begins to receive signals from the spiritual realm that start to interfere with our old I-think-I-feel-I-want way of life. It takes some time for us to get used to listening. It takes even longer to get used to actually doing what we hear; to begin to walk by the Spirit in *oneness* with our Creator.

The process of learning to live with an awakened spirit often feels like an internal war. The apostle, Paul, spoke of the battle numerous times as he corresponded with various churches. In his letter to the Romans, for example, he described it this way:

> "For I know that nothing good dwells in me, that is, in my flesh. For I have the desire to do what is right, but not the ability to carry it out. For I do not do the good I want, but the evil I do not want is what I keep on doing." [26]

Notice that Paul uses the term, "flesh." That is the term the Bible uses to describe partnership between soul and body. It is that unholy partnership that resists so consistently our attempts to listen, trust and obey the voice of the Father via our enlivened spirit. In another letter, this time to the Galatians, Paul writes:

> But I say, walk by the Spirit, and you will not gratify the desires of the flesh. For the desires of the flesh are against the Spirit, and the desires of the Spirit are against the flesh, for these are

opposed to each other, to keep you from doing
the things you want to do. [27]

Nevertheless, that opposition in our lives is necessary if we are to learn submission and gain the advantage of being of one mind with God again.

In our city, September is the end of summer vacation for children of school age. After school resumes in the fall, many students spend their after-class hours outside practicing for fall sports. There are playgrounds and fields reserved for drills and scrimmages. In a way, marriage is the practice field for learning submission, the skill that is needed to re-enter the "oneness" relationship with God. In the context of relationship we learn how to walk as one, and the more we do, the more comfortable we become with the relationship; and the more aware we are when the relationship with our spouse or with God, is weakened by careless, selfish behavior.

Moreover, as we get stronger in the walk of the Spirit, we take the first steps toward making an impact for the kingdom of God in the world. We sense a new closeness to God that begins to attract us and awakens in us a desire to worship, which is to present our bodies as a "living sacrifice, holy and acceptable to God."[28] The outcome of that encounter is humility, the recognition that we are utterly dependent on the Father for our life and purpose. As we grow in humility, we are able to walk in unity, that vital quality that brings us to maturity and prepares us to serve. From unity we are prepared for community, first in our marital relationship, and then to the community of the church. If we are diligent to walk toward that kind of oneness, we are being made ready to make an impact on our world.

Homework Assignments

1. Begin building your "Top 100 Do, Be, Have List" by working on the Life List Exercise below.

2. Ask your spouse: "What can I do to bring you joy today?"

3. Make a list of five things you would like to accomplish in the next twelve months. Indicate which ones are the most important to you.

4. Compare your list of goals with your spouse's list. How are they similar? Where do they differ? What mechanism have you used in the past to prioritize these things?

5. If you have time, select one or more goals and list the strategic steps you must take to accomplish them.

Life List Exercise

This exercise helps a couple share their dreams, hopes and desires in a way that promotes dialog, teamwork and purpose. Follow the instructions until you are quite familiar with the process, then adapt it for your relationship.

Getting Started

1. List at least 100 things you would be willing to do, be or have.

2. Review the list and scratch out anything you don't really want.

3. Pick the top ten items from the remaining list.

4. Compare your top ten with that of your spouse, and merge the lists.

5. Prioritize the items on the combined list:
- Things we are required to do, be or have (Matthew 6:25-26).

- Things that would make our life better, but not required (Matt 7:11).
- Things we would enjoy as part of a dream or desire (Psalm 37:4; 1 Timothy 6:17).
- Things we can hardly imagine (Ephesians 3:20).

Goal Setting Process

1. Brainstorm together about your plans, goals and dreams.
2. Verify that the plans and goals are for US (not you + me).
3. Prioritize goals and plans by time and resources.
4. List your goals (objectives) for the coming year.
5. Arrange the remaining objectives into future phases.

Progress and Praise

1. Review and renew your list semi-annually.
2. Schedule a "date night" at least quarterly to check on progress.
3. Agree together on the next action item.
4. Celebrate successes (Phil 4:4).

Chapter 2

Covenant

Marriage is God's Picture of Covenant

As we suggested in the last chapter, the condition of oneness that we are called to is to be a picture of the nature and character of God. It goes even deeper than that, though. The relationship between a husband and wife not only describes the nature of God, it is a prophetic picture of God's intention for all of history.

That's a bold statement. Wedding as prophecy? To clarify that statement, we are going to insert an excerpt from Dan and Jody's book, *Sword of Submission*: [1]

A Prophetic Image

[My] daughter, Corrie, looked breathtaking on her wedding day. I had seen her in the bride's room before the ceremony; nevertheless, when she appeared at the back of the church, her father by her side, I was struck by how beautiful she looked—positively luminous. The months of anticipation were finally over. The romance that had begun while Corrie was away at college had blossomed and now, surrounded by family and friends, the couple was about to enter into a lifelong covenant. The congregation stood. As Scottish pipes played a haunting melody, Corrie moved down the aisle. When she reached the front of the auditorium, Dan, who also officiated, spoke a blessing, then ascended the platform and began the ceremony.

Visualize the moment. The bride, radiant in her spotless gown, waits at the foot of the stairs. The bridegroom waits for his cue to descend and escort his bride to her father...

Freeze frame.

Let's consider this image for a moment. It is a prophetic glimpse of the future of the followers of [Jesus], Christ's bride who is growing in submission as she awaits her bridegroom.

Beginning with the wedding feast at Cana, much of what Jesus taught about the kingdom was couched in wedding imagery, including some of his most beloved words:

> Let not your heart be troubled; believe in God, believe also in Me. In My Father's house are many dwelling places; if it were not so, I would have told you; for I go to prepare a place for you. And if I go and prepare a place for you, I will come again, and receive you to Myself; that where I am, there you may be also. [2]

In Jesus' time, after a couple became engaged it was common for the bridegroom to return to his father's estate to prepare a home for his future bride. The process could take a year or more. Once everything was ready, he would come back to the bride's home, typically at night, to fetch his bride. Surrounded by blazing torches and celebration, the betrothed couple with their friends and family, would make a joyous procession to his father's house, the place of the festivities.

Now, let's return to that day at the church.

The groom descends from the platform to claim his bride. The bride, having made herself ready for this moment, receives her groom. Together, they ascend the stairs and stand before the father. The significance of that picture should not be overlooked. Every Christian couple on their wedding day stands as a living reminder of the destiny of the race that the Creator placed in the dimension of time and space.

Based on that picture, Jesus plays the role of "the eternal Bridegroom" who is preparing a place for his "eternal bride," the church, and will return for her at the appointed time. Paul describes the event in a letter he wrote to the Christ followers in Thessalonica:

> For the Lord Himself will descend from heaven with a shout, with the voice of the archangel, and with the trumpet of God; and the dead in Christ shall rise first. Then we who are alive and remain shall be caught up together with them in the clouds to meet the Lord in the air, and thus we shall always be with the Lord. [3]

The stage is set. For two millennia Paul's description has been alive in the soul of the church. As she waits, anticipating the coming of her Lord, the anxious bride—his people—makes preparations for that day. Through the indwelling Holy Spirit who has resurrected the once dead human spirit, God's people are learning submission so they can rediscover the joy of being cherished children, loved and disciplined; valued servants, bought with a price; and, at last, a bride, betrothed and beloved.

Furthermore, the Christian practice of baptism has similar qualities to a wedding ceremony because it is a public declaration of the devotion of a new believer to Christ as savior and Lord; the entry of a person into the church. It, too, is a declaration of covenant. Dan will often use the traditional wedding vows during a baptism to describe the action being taken by the new believer: "Will you have Jesus as your savior and Lord? To have and to hold from this day forward; for better for worse, for richer or for poorer, for now and forever?"

That a Christian wedding (and baptism) is a prophetic picture emphasizes the importance of the oneness principle. Moreover, it invites us to take a closer look at the bond between a husband and a wife. Let's start with an image that stands as a humorous contrast to the wedding picture above.

Contracts and Covenants

It seemed like such a great idea at the time. It was to be a creative and romantic way to ask her to marry him: return to the park where they first met and buy her a helium balloon, just as he had on that gorgeous day when love took wing. Only this time he would tie an engagement ring to the balloon, present it to her, drop to one knee and "pop the question," all while a friend captured the magic moment on video.

The video recording preserves everything perfectly. The future bridegroom strolls up to his beloved; he gives her the bright red balloon and gallantly kneels. She squeals with delight, and puts her hands to her mouth...and lets go of the balloon ... which sails upward.

The horrified boyfriend leaps to his feet and lunges for the balloon. "Wait! Wait! Oh, no!"

"What!?" cries the startled, almost fiancée, as she watches her future husband sprinting and leaping, vainly trying to catch the balloon and its diamond payload.

"Oh, no! The ring! It's tied to the balloon!"

"What?" she shrieks again. "Why did you do that?"

He is still sprinting, but it's too late. "I don't know. I thought it would be romantic. Somebody call the fire department or something..."

Bye-bye love. Bye-bye romance that might have been. [4]

Sometimes it seems that love is as fleeting as that balloon. What can be done to keep marriages solid and our relationship from slipping through our fingers? What keeps us grounded in our commitment, our hearts tethered firmly together and to God?

The word that God uses to describe unbreakable relationships is *covenant*. It describes an association that is quite different than a relationship that is merely "contractual."

A definition might be useful here. A contract is a legal arrangement that seeks to secure the greatest benefit for each party to it. At the same time, it is meant to limit the liability of the parties. In other words, a contract is designed to protect the personal interests of everybody involved. Everybody is looking out for themselves—the parties hold each other to the terms of the contract. If the terms are violated at any point, the contract becomes null and void. The relationship, like the balloon in the illustration, becomes less and less secure until it slips away and the contract is broken.

But that's different than a covenant. Let's not forget that a covenant is what God had in mind when he created human beings. "Covenant" is the terminology he chose to describe His relationship with us. We've already seen that we were created so that through our interpersonal relationships, especially our marriages, we can understand Him better. Then it's clear that our marriage is more than a contract. It is a covenant.

When God strikes a covenant, He does it for the benefit of *another*, since it can hardly be said that it benefits Him. As He enters into a relationship with His creation, our part of the bargain is to reflect that same selflessness back at Him and toward the others in our lives, first of all our marriage partner. This is what Jesus meant when He said, "be perfect, as your heavenly Father is perfect." The word, "perfect" isn't to be understood as a condition of flawlessness, but as maturity in that quality Jesus had been describing, namely a selfless attitude toward others. A covenant is an arrangement that is to reflect God's grace upon us.

When it is acted out in a marriage, it is an arrangement that seeks the mutual benefit of the parties involved. It not only takes responsibility to the benefit of the other ("to love, comfort, honor and keep"), it assumes liability ("for better or worse; in sickness and in health; for richer and for poorer"). Unlimited responsibility. Unlimited liability. Both extended by each party in the relationship toward the other. That is covenant.

It is a New Covenant, which is the fulfillment of the covenant that was in place before Jesus Christ. The Old Covenant was performance based. Sacrifice and human effort were combined to create a relationship with God. But that Old Covenant was preparation for the new one. What initially looked like a system of rules to control people was really the prequel to the story of redemption. It was pointing to Jesus and the coming of the Holy Spirit who would change people fundamentally—what once bound people by rules would change them by the grace of God.

The contrast between the old and new gets clearer as we look at Jesus' response to a challenge from an expert in the Old Covenant law.

> And one of them ... asked him a question to test him: "Teacher, which commandment in the law is the greatest?" Jesus said to him," 'Love the Lord your God with all your heart, with all your soul, and with all your mind.' This is the first and greatest commandment. The second is like it: 'Love your neighbor as yourself.' All the law and the prophets depend on these two commandments." [5]

So, was Jesus' answer speaking of the Old or New Covenant? Jesus simply answered the question that the lawyer was asking, a question based on the Old Covenant. And the Old Covenant answer? Love the Lord with all you have.

Throw yourself into it. Try. Try and try harder. But elsewhere, in what is called "the sermon on the mount," Jesus explains the New Covenant.

"Do not think that I have come to abolish the law or the prophets. I have not come to abolish these things but to fulfill them. I tell you the truth, until heaven and earth pass away not the smallest letter or stroke of a letter will pass from the law until everything takes place. So anyone who breaks one of the least of these commands and teaches others to do so will be called least in the kingdom of heaven, but whoever obeys them and teaches others to do so will be called great in the kingdom of heaven. For I tell you, unless your righteousness goes beyond that of the experts in the law and the Pharisees, you will never enter the kingdom of heaven. You have heard that it was said to an older generation, 'Do not murder,' and 'whoever murders will be subjected to judgment.' But I say to you that anyone who is angry with a brother will be subjected to judgment. And whoever insults a brother will be brought before the council, and whoever says 'Fool' will be sent to fiery hell. So then, if you bring your gift to the altar and there remember that your brother has something against you, leave your gift there in front of the altar. First go and be reconciled to your brother and then come and present your gift. Reach agreement quickly with your accuser while on the way to court, or he may hand you over to the judge, and the judge hand you over to the warden, and you will be thrown into prison. I tell you the truth, you will never get out of there until you have paid the last penny! You have heard that it was said, 'Do not commit adultery.' But I say to you that whoever looks at a woman to desire her has already committed adultery with her in his heart." [6]

Notice that Jesus doesn't disregard the old law. His goal is to cause it to have some kind of result. It's not about rule-keeping and intense effort—giving it all we have. It's about allowing God, by His Spirit, to change us. Then the law will have achieved its full purpose.

As an illustration, think of a measuring cup. Whether glass, metal or plastic you'll find one in most kitchens, a pitcher-like container with markings up the side indicating the amount of liquid or dry ingredient it contains. The chef may fill it partly full—a quarter or a half—but if it is filled to capacity, it has fulfilled the maximum purpose for which it was designed.

Jesus is telling His listeners that God forbids murder and that God wrote that into His law. But to be able to say you haven't killed anyone only means you have kept the law; it doesn't mean you have fulfilled it. God gave the law so we would clearly understand His heart on the subject of taking someone's life. But having understood His heart, has our own heart begun to reflect His? Have we rejected anger toward others, which is the seed of murder? That is the law fulfilled.

The same is true concerning adultery. God clearly states that he forbids unfaithfulness in marriage. It violates the covenant. Jesus says that adultery doesn't begin with the outward act of unfaithfulness, but in a person's heart. The "adulterous heart" is a sign of unfulfilled law. When a believer recognizes the impure thought in himself, the law that has been fulfilled causes conviction and repentance resulting in an intentional redirection of thinking. Our willingness to respond to conviction in the private space between our ears is New Covenant, the law fulfilled, and a heart that has begun to reflect the heart of the Father.

Outrageous Love

When Jesus came along, He changed everything. His teaching set up the transition from old to new, then His crucifixion blew open the door to a different way of life. That new life reflects a New Covenant answer to the Great Commandment. Remember what it said: love the Lord your God with all you have—heart, soul and mind.

Now consider the new commandment from the lips of Jesus:

> I give you a new commandment — to love one another. Just as I have loved you, you also are to love one another. Everyone will know by this that you are my disciples — if you have love for one another. [7]

Here, Jesus calls his followers to take action by loving others. He uses His own self-sacrificing, covenant love as the pattern, which distinguishes what He is talking about from the Old Covenant. Old love is worked out in the time and space dimension. It starts with us as the source and initiator. "New commandment" love is initiated from the eternal side of things. It is the completion of the Great Commandment of the law: Do acts of love for others, even in spite of their shortcomings; not because we feel inclined to, but because it benefits another. Unlimited responsibility. Unlimited liability.

That sounds like a tall order. And it is. That is why it requires new life in the Holy Spirit to do it. Jesus' disciples were not to be old creatures striving to love; they were to be new creatures expressing His love. We aren't to be the producers of love, giving it all we have; we are the delivery system for the covenant love of God. This love from heaven is the means by which our Creator intends to "destroy the works of the devil." [8] The apostle, John, described it like this:

> So we have come to know and to believe the love that God has for us. God is love, and whoever abides in love abides in God, and God abides in him. By this is love perfected with us, so that we may have confidence for the Day of Judgment, because as [Jesus] is so also are we in this world. There is no fear in love, but perfect love casts out fear. For fear has to do with punishment, and whoever fears has not been perfected in love. We love because he first loved us. [9]

What outrageous love! It invites us to walk in fearless confidence that we are loved by God and then to reflect that love back on the others in our life. It's a way of life that we have to learn; it doesn't come all at once. But our Father intends to progressively draw us into it and then release it through us. It is intimate and relational, like marriage and it is effective to bring transformation to anyone who is willing to be shaped by it.

What better place for that shaping to occur than in the covenant of marriage.

Understanding Oaths and Vows

The active ingredient in a marriage ceremony is the exchange of vows. The moment is recognizable by the initiating phrase "Do you ..." and concluding comment: "I do." Somewhere in this exchange promises are made or affirmed, and two people are committed according to the conditions set forth.

It is a spiritual transaction.

Whether a person understands the implications or not, a covenant has been established that is binding in the spiritual realm. The legal ramifications are important here on earth, but the eternal impact is much more significant. We need to understand it from God's perspective, since this truth overrides our feelings or expectations.

An oath is a promise I make to myself that is attested to by a witness. The promise is binding on me and by me. The authority of the witness determines the strength of the promise, and establishes the source of punishment should the promise be broken. The risk of an oath is to make a promise that cannot be kept, and to invoke a witness over whom you do not have authority. This is the reason Jesus taught that you should not take an oath at all. [10]

A vow is a promise I make to another person that is attested to by a witness. Similar to an oath, the authority of the witness determines the strength of the promise and source of punishment if it is broken.

A marriage is built on a promise, or vow, between two willing and able people. The audience acts as unofficial witness, able to attest to the historicity of the event. Legally, the promise is witnessed by two or more participants in the wedding party (traditionally the best man and maid of honor) who declare that the bride and groom are making these promises without coercion. The officiant (minister) acts as witness for the government. This makes the agreement both legally and historically binding.

The promise is anchored to truth by its authority. When God made His promise to Abraham, He swore by Himself since there was no one greater for Him to swear by. Because He wanted to make the unchanging nature of the promise very clear, He confirmed it with an oath.[11] In other words, God's promise will come true because it is His will, and there is no one with higher authority able to override it.

Men swear by someone greater than themselves to confirm what is said and put an end to all argument. There is still opportunity for argument, but the witness determines the realm of the argument. For instance, if I swear by God then there is no place for argument except by God. Alternatively, if I swear by myself then I must defend it myself. Again, if I swear by the law then the promise is argued and defended by the law. The authority of the witness establishes credibility and anchors the truth.

The highest authority is God. The character and nature of God is perfect and unchangeable, therefore His witness is irrefutable.

Jesus warned about making oaths and vows because they are spiritual transactions. God created man in His own image and we reflect His character and attributes. Since God's promises are binding, ours are as well. All of God's promises are perfect and binding. But we have fallen into sin, and in our sinful nature we may make imperfect promises that are binding because of our godly nature.

The spoken word is powerful for the same reason: we are created in His image. God spoke and all things were created out of nothing. He speaks things into existence, and when He proclaims a promise He creates its outcome. Our godly nature means we have prophetic speech, too. Our sinful nature means we can speak evil things into existence.

Jesus taught us about the use of statements and confession because of this great power in words. When we confess something, we are stating it as it is. We confess our sins and fears so Jesus can forgive them. This might be considered the negative side of confession. Positive confession is to speak the truth. For example, when we confess Jesus as Lord it speaks that truth into us and into our surroundings. It is as if we are speaking our faith into existence.

What we say and how we say it is that important. When we are making a promise, speaking an oath or a vow, it creates a binding condition on us. If we also invoke the character of God on that promise, we are declaring it to be in His image.

Our promises take on the character of God, so they are unchanging, eternal and true. We are assigning His power and authority to this promise.

There are some that do not regard God as the highest authority in their life. They are not living under His authority, but under a substitutionary authority instead. There is some kind of code in their lives, but they are not being aligned with God's character: eternal, objective, universal, loving, and infinite. Their promises will not be regarded with these characteristics either.

The book of Judges describes the nation of Israel at the time when they had no king by saying: "Everyone did what was right in their own eyes." It still happens today with anyone that substitutes themselves for God as their highest authority. They are aligned with their own character: temporal, subjective, capricious, self-centered, and limited in scope. Their promises also follow these characteristics.

God frequently and fervently warned against idolatry in the Law and Prophets, and any substitute for His authority is an idol. Consider the character and nature of false gods and the devil and you will discover the foundational influence in the lives and promises of many people. They become evil, accusers, isolated and restricted, and their promises are as well.

Intentional Oaths and Vows

There are many places in our culture where we properly engage in oaths or vows, such as courts of law, marriages, legal proceedings, and some group memberships. These promises are made intentionally; they are entered into by free will.

There are two major considerations in our culture regarding the validity of such promises. First, they must be given by someone with a sound mind. In other words, the person must be capable of making that decision in light of the consequences. Secondly, they must do so freely. If someone is forced or coerced into making the promise there is no certainty that they did it willingly, thereby binding them to it.

The authority under which the promise is made is also selected by the free will of the person making it. For example, when a boy scout swears, "On my honor, I will do my best to do my duty ...," his promise is invoking personal authority. His promise is confirmed by himself and invokes all the character and strength of himself.

On the other hand, a witness in a courtroom in the United States will be asked: "Do you swear to tell the truth ...so help you God?" Traditionally this was to signify that the person's oath was witnessed by God. The worldview of our country has changed over the years and it is not regarded as an oath under God any longer. It is more accurate to say that this oath is made under the authority of the legal system. To obey the oath is the responsibility of the person and the punishment of disobedience is meted out by the courts.

We have a friend that gave his life to the Lord as a young man. He acknowledges God as the highest authority in his life, and made an oath by which he promised himself to God. He also made a vow to raise his children under God in the same way. This vow is binding on him and God, because God promises that He will receive our children and cover them in His covenant. This is an important and powerful step to be taken by a father.

His son is choosing to live in rebellion against God and the truth. As he became independent, he has broken allegiance with God and declares that he no longer believes in Him and will not follow in His ways. His free will breaks the promise his father made with God, and thereby loses the protection of that promise. He has chosen to make an oath to the devil instead, promising to live his life according to spirits and influences that oppose God. It is a poignant demonstration of love that God allows him to choose, even if it means death instead of life.

This young man married and became a father. He named his first daughter Persephone. In Greek mythology, Persephone is described as the daughter of Zeus and Demeter; she was abducted by Hades and became the queen of the underworld. Choosing this name indicates the vow under which this child is being raised. Her father has extended his oath to her.

Notice the generational impact of oaths and vows. God's love does not override a person's free will, but the promises made and kept have a dramatic influence for good or evil on the predisposition of your children before they reach maturity.

The person that makes an intentional oath or vow is able to revoke it by appealing to a higher authority.

In the above example the first father made a vow to God by his authority as a father. His son broke that promise by appealing to a higher authority, in this case his own free will. While he was a minor, under the authority of his father, his choices were subject to his father. When he became independent he began to operate under his own authority. He appealed to his independent authority, exercised his free will, and revoked the vow his father had made. He revoked it by entering into a new oath that superseded it.

Even now, if he were to repent of his ways, he could revoke the oath he made to the devil by appealing to a higher authority. The Higher Authority is God, and a new vow or oath made to Him would supersede the prior ones. It requires confession of the original promise and a request for forgiveness. Then God releases the person from their sin and as a new creation they are able to enter into a new agreement.

Persephone will also have the ability to revoke the vow placed on her. When she becomes independent from her father, she will be able to exercise her God-given free will to revoke the vow and replace it with an oath to God as her higher authority.

It is likely that you have intentionally made an oath or vow inappropriately, and by the conviction of the Holy Spirit you realize that you must revoke that promise. Perhaps you made a promise without realizing the entailments, or you swore by God or yourself to build you own sense of conviction or to convince someone else of your sincerity. Revoke these promises as the Holy Spirit brings them to mind.

The highest authority is God, and one of His chief characteristics is truth. This truth comes through Jesus. In John 8:32 it says: "And you will know the truth, and the truth will set you free." The freedom comes as you are released from the oath by appealing to the truth. It goes on to say in verse 36: "So if the Son sets you free, you will be free indeed." These are the promises we can claim, and they are useful to us when we come to realize we have placed ourselves in a position of obligation.

Unintentional Oaths and Vows

There are other times when we stumble into an oath or vow quite unintentionally. It is still a matter of free will, but you made the choice while under the influence of some other force. Temptation and deception are two of the biggest factors in unintentional oaths, because the devil wants to use promises as legal ground and leverage for control. Another factor can be ignorance, where a person is unaware of oaths, vows and the power they hold. Unfortunately, ignorance is not a defense against the consequences of the law.

The authority invoked by an unintentional oath or vow is established by default. In other words, most promises will be made under the authority generally recognized by the person. If they normally regard themselves as their highest authority, then that is the authority they have appealed to for the promise. Also, if there is a generally accepted authority with that particular promise, then that becomes the authority under which the promise is made. In that case, an oath in a courtroom would be under the legal system's authority by default.

We had a young man, twenty-four years old, come to us for prayer ministry. He was fighting to overcome alcoholism and drug addiction, and to move forward in his life. He had anxiety about providing for his family, difficulty holding down a job, and reluctance to commit to anything new. He had recommitted his life to the Lord a year before, and things were better but not great. He needed help.

I was prompted by the Holy Spirit to ask if there was any legal ground that the devil might be using to thwart his progress. After some discussion, we went to prayer. The Holy Spirit called to his mind an unintentional oath.

He shared this: "I was twelve years old. My dad had to spend a year in prison and it was hard on the family. My grandpa had suffered from Parkinson's disease, and then died that year. We had been praying about these things, and it didn't seem to make any difference. It wasn't fair. I remember going for a walk by myself one night, and I was mad at God. 'I will never trust You again!' I yelled."

That was an oath. He had promised himself that he would never trust God again. When I explained the conditions of his promise he was deeply sorry. He could attest to the truth of the bind he was in, and assumed it was just weak faith. For years he had tried to believe, but immediately the devil swooped in to accuse him by using the legal ground of the promise and holding him to it: "You cannot trust God, because you promised you would never trust Him again!"

I led him in a prayer to confess this unintentional oath to God, and ask for forgiveness. He confessed and repented, and felt the peace of forgiveness flood into his heart. At my instruction, he replaced that oath with an intentional promise to follow God and trust Him in all His ways. We then declared the original oath to be null and void, replaced by this promise to God, and recognized Him as the Highest Authority. This young man's life began to change that very day, and it was obvious to all who knew him.

Notice the steps we took to revoke the unintentional oath because it works the same for unintentional vows. First, you must recognize that your promise was made amiss, and choose to make amends. Submit yourself, and the promise, to God as the Highest Authority. Use your free will to choose to change. Claim God's promise that He will forgive your sin when you confess it to Him.[12] Then stand on His truth in place of whatever authority you used.

There is incredible power in the spoken word. When we speak, because we are created in God's image, we speak creation or we speak re-creation into existence. God created by speaking, and His words are life.[13] Because we are fallen, we can speak curses and death. It is the prophetic power of words, for good or evil. This is no trifling matter, but a severe warning so that you will use this power carefully.

We will explore this power in greater depth as we talk about the power of words for blessings and curses in your marriage. In every aspect of your life, what you say is potent. That is why Jesus warned that you will give an account for every careless word (Matthew 12:36).

Revisiting Your Marriage Vows

You made a covenant contract when you got married. It is a vow that you entered into intentionally, and it has significant impact on your life. It is a spiritual transaction that binds you in ways that go well beyond the legal and traditional expectations of your culture. God cares about it.

Think about when you got married. Your vows were exchanged under some authority. Perhaps they were given in respect to the legal authority of the state in which you got married. In a country where approximately half of marriages end in divorce, the legal system has a poor track record for authority.

Alternatively, you may have acknowledged only yourselves as your authority. For some people, that means they are making a promise based on their own character, and they don't even trust themselves. They are making promises they really have no intention of keeping. For example, have you known anyone that signed a pre-nuptial agreement before getting married? They make a legally binding agreement about how they will separate, while at the same time they are making a legally binding agreement to stay together forever. How ironic is that?

It is time to consider the promises you made. Whether you operated in complete understanding or complete ignorance, the words you spoke represent a spiritual transaction. They are powerful in the heavenly realms, for blessing you or cursing you. The enemy will not miss an opportunity to use your words against you and hold you to improper promises.

God is beyond time, and He can sanctify and redeem the decisions that we made. He can do this retroactively.

I (Calvin) have asked men this question: "If you had it all to do over again, knowing what you know now, would you choose to marry your wife? Knowing all the good things that happened that were better than you expected; but also knowing everything that turned out worse than you expected, would you choose her?"

The right answer is "yes." It becomes the right answer as we celebrate and thank God for everything that turned out better than we expected, and as we forgive each other for everything that turned out worse than we expected. These are the practical steps of sanctifying and redeeming the past.

My follow up question to men is this: "What would it take for you to go back in time and choose her? What can you do today to sanctify and redeem your relationship?"

Take a step back in time with me to the first of June in 1978. In a crowded sanctuary I stand in a powder blue tuxedo, gazing at my beautiful girlfriend. I speak in halting voice these words of promise:

"Julie, in the presence of God and before our relatives and friends, I take you to be my wife. I will love you with tenderness and respect, sharing myself with you physically, emotionally and spiritually and I will encourage you to develop God's gifts in you, as long as our lives shall last."

We wrote these vows together in the weeks before our wedding. They were crafted after many conversations and discussions about what we were actually promising each other. It was an intentional effort, engaged in with all seriousness. If I were to renew my vow to my wife today, I would not change a word.

Consider the promises you made, particularly in light of the seriousness of vows and oaths. What words did you speak? How intentional were you? All the words you used have power, and you will be required to give an account for each of them.

Under whose authority did you make your vows? If you got married in a church, it may have been implied that you were doing so under the authority of God. But consider who you recognized as the authority. Ask yourself who reigned as the highest authority in your life at that time.

Did you make your vows under the Old Covenant? If so, your power is based on your efforts and ability. You are depending on all your best efforts, strong self-control, and proper performance. Or did you make your vows under the New Covenant, the love of God compelling and empowering you to achieve His will? Now is the time to ratify your marriage, and if you have been operating under any authority besides God as the Highest Authority, then appeal to Him.

Men and women are susceptible to second guessing their commitment to each other. They wonder if this was really the person they were supposed to marry. Often they admit that they married out of fear, or that this would be their only chance. Sometimes they admit to feeling a check in their spirit before getting married, a nudge from the Holy Spirit to indicate that this was not the right one. Yet, they plunged ahead out of fear, embarrassment, or rebellion. They may see their vows as a millstone tied around their neck, and are hoping for a loophole through which they can escape.

We have encountered some that are looking for a Christian way out, wondering how they can hit a reset button or invoke an "undo" command. Our encouragement to them is that God does not have an undo, reset, or loophole for them, but if they are willing to trust Him, a miracle can redeem and sanctify the vows and the marriage. This is true even for those that ignored the Holy Spirit's prompting and married anyway.

Renew Your Vows

How well have you performed? Have you kept your promises? Whether under God's authority or your own, you may have promised to forsake all others. You may have promised to love and cherish in sickness or in health, for richer or poorer, in thick and thin. A broken promise is not the loophole through which a vow is excused.

Broken promises can be restored. It is done in an intentional act, initiated by the one that broke the vow and performed for the one to whom the promise was made. Step one is to confess the breach to the other in sorrow and ask for forgiveness. The offended party has the right to forgive the debt. Upon being forgiven, the debtor is able to repent, which means to change their behavior in accordance with the new start they have been given. We will cover the topic of forgiveness in greater depth in a later chapter, but do not wait to initiate the conversations that lead to repentance.

Remember that under the first covenant we are guilty of not being able to keep the law, which leads to death. We have received the promised eternal inheritance because Jesus died in our place.[14] It takes death to pay for our indiscretions of broken covenant. If you are the one that needs to forgive the transgression of your spouse, then remember that Jesus died for his or her sin as well.

Under the Old Covenant of the law we are doomed, but Jesus obeyed that law and established a New Covenant.[15] Because of His obedience, He was qualified to make a new one. As you have seen, the New Covenant is made on the promise of life, and the exchange of sanctification for sin. In your marriage, you can invoke this New Covenant by receiving sanctification in place of your sin by the same agency of transferral to Jesus. It is an intentional choice, entered into by mutual agreement between two parties. It redeems the poor performance of the past and establishes a new order for performance in the future.

As you revisit your vows, choose to establish a New Covenant. Jesus said: "A new commandment I give to you, that you love one another: just as I have loved you, you are to love one another."[16] This is the basis of the renewed vows you promise each other.

Repair your vows if they have been broken or spoken amiss. Husbands, this is your opportunity to choose your wife all over again. Wives, this is your opportunity to be chosen and receive your husband all over again. Rebuild your marriage on a covenant of love and forgiveness, as Jesus has done with you.

Ambassadors are representatives of their homeland on foreign soil. We are called to be ambassadors of reconciliation.[17] We do this through our marriage by representing our homeland: heaven. God's picture of reconciliation and love flows down from Him to you, and from you to your spouse, and from you as a couple outward to others. It is vital that your relationship be reconciled so that a searching world will have a physical representation by which they can understand God.

Renew your vows and accept a redeemed covenant. A covenant provides protection based on the conditions set forth, and established by the authority of its maker. A broken covenant removes that protection and allows judgment to affect the separated party. Let God's covenant protect you and be manifested through you.

Can you think of a good way to signify that renewed covenant? Here's a suggestion. Do what we do in an actual Marriage Rx session: share the Lord's Table—bread and cup— together as a couple.

Celebrate Communion

The first step in a Jewish marriage is the betrothal, which is really the establishment of the covenant. The bridegroom traveled to the bride's family home and negotiated a bridal price (mohar) with her father. The covenant was binding between the man and woman when the price was paid. Always ready for a party, the families would throw a celebration dinner for the extended family.

The highlight of the evening was the cup of blessing. Near the end of the dinner the host, or an honored guest, would pronounce a blessing over a cup of wine. For this dinner celebration he would give a betrothal blessing, proclaiming good things for their life together. Everyone cheered as the betrothed couple received that blessing by drinking from a shared cup.

Imagine the surprise and confusion the disciples experienced in the upper room during the Last Supper. The last cup of the Seder dinner represented the fourth way God redeemed Israel: "I will take you to be My people, and I will be your God." and was accompanied with the Hallel psalms (115-118). The symbolism of redemption and marriage were completely intermingled. The blessing Jesus pronounced over the cup was unmistakably a betrothal blessing. Then He made this proposal:

"Drink of it, all of you, for this is My blood of the covenant, which is poured out for many for the forgiveness of sins."

Drink and you declare that you are accepting His proposal. You become His bride and are forever accepted into His family. His blood was poured out for a complete remission of all your sins, and by faith in Him you become righteous.

Homework Assignments

Celebrate Communion Together

Prepare the elements for your communion service that represent the bread and wine like Jesus offered the disciples. Take a moment together to share what His proposal means to you. Consider together the ramifications of being married to Him, as well as to each other. Remember that this is a replication of the trinity pattern: God, husband, and wife as a cord of three strands that is not easily broken.

When you share the bread, remember the words of Jesus: "This is My body which is for you. Do this in remembrance of Me." His body was broken for your salvation.

When you share the wine, remember the words of Jesus: "This cup is the New Covenant in My blood. Do this, as often as you drink it, in remembrance of Me." His blood was shed for a complete remission of all your sin.

Pray together for direction from the Holy Spirit; listen for guidance on how to restore your covenant to Him and each other. If He convicts you of any sin, confess it to Him and ask for forgiveness. Receive His righteousness individually and together and be sanctified.

Marriage Rx

Chapter 3

Naked and Unashamed

Hiding from God and Each Other

If it weren't so tragic, the story of the Garden of Eden would have been funny—part of it, anyway. You remember the story. There in the garden, Adam and Eve had it made in the shade. Everything they needed was there for them. Even the climate was perfect. We know that because the last verse of Genesis 2 tells us, "And the man and his wife were both naked and were not ashamed."

Notice that they were unashamed together, thoroughly enjoying their environment. They had good attitudes and a positive relationship. Not only that, they had a great relationship with their Creator who would drop by for a visit from time to time. Imagine! A social call from God!

The only restriction our first parents had to endure was to abstain from a particular tree in the midst of the garden: the tree of the knowledge of good and evil. That tree, according to God, was to be avoided because if they ate from it they would surely die—a dire warning if there ever was one.

It may be worth noting here, though, that when it came to knowledge, there was really only one kind of knowledge that tree had to offer, the knowledge of evil. Adam and Eve were already well acquainted with good. Everything God made—their whole world—was good. No, the only thing that being disobedient could possibly offer was evil; bad news.

It's no surprise, then, that something bad happens when our first parents act against God's instruction. The evidence that things in the world have changed for the worse is found in Genesis 3:7.

> Then the eyes of both of them were opened, and they knew that they were naked. And they sewed fig leaves together and made for themselves loincloths.

Before, they had wandered around their safe and perfect environment naked and unashamed; now, having eaten from the tree of knowledge, that was changed. They were suddenly ashamed, and had the urge to cover up. The issue wasn't a sudden realization that they had nothing on. They were smart enough to know that. What was new was shame, wanting to put some sort of covering or barrier over themselves. And not only to hide from each other. Look at verse eight:

> And they heard the sound of the LORD God walking in the garden in the cool of the day, and the man and his wife hid themselves from the presence of the LORD God among the trees of the garden. But the LORD God called to the man and said to him, "Where are you?"

Here, God drops by for one of His customary visits. Where are His children? Why don't they come, eagerly to greet Him? Because they are ashamed. They are victims of their own sin. Because of pride, they thought they could get something for themselves that God was unwilling to give them. Now, they have become self-centered, more concerned for their own shame than for their relationship with their Creator or with each other. The first sign that evil had entered the world was pride, then shame, then isolation. Moreover, their attitude toward God was diminished. They actually thought they could hide from their omniscient Creator, who reveals their folly to them when He asks a question: Where are you?

Indeed. Where were they? God didn't ask the question because He didn't know their whereabouts. He asked it because they needed to face the reality of their sin. They had withdrawn from relationship, having turned from the gift of God.

God's Good Gift

The topic of intimacy frequently needs to be addressed when we do marriage restoration work. The problem is not a shortage of nakedness. Our culture is full of nakedness. The problem is that nakedness leads to shame. Sin has corrupted our perception of this good gift of God.

Adam and Eve were created in God's image, both male and female. It is the perfect replication of the trinity pattern, and an exact representation of the relationship of God to God, yet ever expanding. God began creating everything from nothing and His assessment of each day's work was that it was good. The conclusion of the first chapter of Genesis sums it up, that on the sixth day God saw that it was very good.

The second chapter of Genesis revisits the creation process with an emphasis on how man was created in God's image. Notice the first occasion in which God says something is not good is that man should be alone. Adam could not reflect the relational character of God without a suitable counterpart.

Now, you would think that the story line would progress from this revelation of conflict directly into its solution. The main character, God, has been introduced as perfect and powerful, so the narrative should record His creative solution to prove it. Yet there is a two verse interruption in the process: Adam is tasked with naming all the animals. We are left hanging, but not because God thinks naming the animals is a higher priority, nor because He is impatient. This exercise is to prove to Adam that no suitable helper could be found among all the created things.

Then the creative solution is revealed: God creates Eve out of Adam's rib! When Adam woke from his deep sleep, he was introduced to his perfect bride and knew that she was "bone of my bone, flesh of my flesh." They were designed *from* one flesh because they were designed *to be* one flesh. God prophetically declares that they will become one as God is One.[1]

> Therefore a man shall leave his father and his mother and hold fast to his wife, and they shall become one flesh. [2]

This is God's description to us of His good gift. The verse describes the man leaving his parents and being joined to his wife, and then proclaims that they become one flesh. This verse is not there for Adam and Eve's benefit, for they didn't have father or mother to leave. It is spoken for us: "A man shall hold fast to his wife and they shall become one flesh." This is speaking of sexual union, an act that binds the two together physically, emotionally and spiritually.

> And the man and his wife were both naked and were not ashamed. [3]

It is no wonder that the man and his wife were naked and not ashamed. There was no reason for shame since each was created in the image of God and perfectly reflected His character. There were no barriers to intimacy. Two separate persons were merged, held fast, and joined into one flesh.

Then came the fall. God had created them complete (very good) with each other and in union with Him, and yet they were tempted by a sense of need. When they reached for a solution outside of themselves and God, it caused a separation of identities. The union of one flesh was broken by that act of dissatisfaction.

Then came the fallout. The unintended consequence of the sin was independence, a separation of self from the union. By choosing the fruit from the Tree of Knowledge, they took on the responsibility to determine for themselves what was good and evil, though they were not designed to carry this burden.

The eyes of both were opened. This means they began to see in a new way. They no longer saw the glory of God reflected accurately through the other. They no longer saw the perfection of how they were designed for each other, or how they fit together. The dissatisfaction fueled insecurity, and suddenly they perceived what was missing rather than what the other was providing. There was an awareness of incompleteness that was no longer resolved.

Mankind is not designed to bear the responsibility of knowing good and evil, and we aren't equipped with an absolute standard by which to judge. Therefore we make our best guesses between good and evil by comparison. Whereas God declared things good or evil, we judge on a relative basis by emphasizing differences.

Imagine Adam and Even when their eyes were opened. Suddenly they saw each other, not as the perfect complement to themselves but as a potential standard for comparison. Judgment was rendered and received between two separated identities that attempted to justify or protect self instead of the union. Each prominent quality observed in one was seen as a comparative failure or weakness in the other.

We see this same pattern expressed in mankind today. It is demonstrated with criticism, condemnation, blaming and shaming. Upon confrontation, Adam blamed Eve ("the woman") first, and God by extension ("You gave me.") Eve shifted the blame to the serpent. These are examples of self protection.

Adam and Eve were naked and unashamed before the fall, but began hiding and blaming immediately after. God's good gift was that they were created from one flesh to be in a one flesh relationship, but sin changed their frame of reference. God gave intimacy and sexual union as a good gift to weld a couple together, but sin wishes to corrupt it with shame and hiding so that it drives a couple apart.

Nakedness has been aligned with shame, and that is a poor substitute for God's good gift.

Lust and Desire

Let's insert a definition here:

> **Desire**: To long or hope for; exhibit or feel desire for; express a wish for; stresses the strength of feeling and often implies strong intention or aim.

This word sounds pretty neutral. All of us know what it is to long for something or to have a strong intention or aim. Often, it is a good thing. To desire to succeed, or to get an education or to wish the best for someone is positive.

Lust, on the other hand, is a different matter. This word carries with it the connotation of something bad. Consider the definition of the word, lust:

> **Lust:** Intense sexual desire or appetite; an over-mastering, excessive craving ; lecherousness..

This word is used in James 1:14-16 in some translations of the Bible.

> ...each person is tempted when he is lured and enticed by his own lust. Then lust when it has conceived gives birth to sin, and sin when it is fully grown brings forth death. Do not be deceived, my beloved brothers.

In other translations, the English Standard Version, for example, guess what word is used: desire. "Each person is tempted when he is lured...by his own *desire*." Why is that the word in one translation when lust is used in another?

It is because the Greek word in the New Testament for 'desire' is the same one that's used to translate the word, 'lust.' The word is, "epithumeo." It means, literally, to have the affections directed toward anything. It can include desire, in a good sense (Matthew 13:17; Luke 22:15; 1 Timothy 3:1), or desire in a natural sense (Luke 15:16; 16:21; 17:22) or to desire in a bad sense (Matthew 5:28; Romans 7:7, 13:9; 1 Corinthians 10:6). When it is used in that negative sense, it may be translated, "lust" or "crave" or "covet."

We are created with the capacity to desire. It is God's means of communing with us. It is good to desire a relationship with God, or to desire to please Him. Human desire is a potent motivator. That is why it needs to be governed, ruled. When human desire is released outside of God's rule and authority it quickly becomes unhealthy—what we call 'lust"—but when it is directed toward obedience to our Creator it becomes powerful.

Contempt for the Body

When our first parents deviated from the loving care of their Creator, something happened to the quality of desire that the human race was able to express. As they turned away from God they turned toward themselves, first in an attempt to elevate their condition by seeking wisdom that God had not offered them, and then toward themselves as an object of shame. That is ironic. They seek wisdom through disobedience and discover evil in the process. Whereas they had been created naked and unashamed, suddenly they reconsidered their condition and attempted to cover themselves, as though who they were had become undesirable—ugly.

That is precisely the opposite assessment from what God had of them in the beginning. Here is what the Bible has to say about God's opinion of creation, including human beings:

> And God saw everything that He had made, and behold, it was very good. And there was evening and there was morning, the sixth day. [4]

And why *wouldn't* God think His human creation was good? After all, the Bible tells us that God made human beings in His image to be a reflection of Him. The man was to display His strength and power;[5] the woman to display God's beauty. [6]

Yet, after their disobedience, Adam and Eve find themselves not only naked and ashamed, but no longer submitted to God, including His assessment of their value and their identity. See where their sin has brought them? Their so-called wisdom has left them to deal with opinions contrary to God's. That is, their own opinions and also the opinions of an evil "accuser" who has poisoned the human family with a toxin we can call "contempt."

Let's consider the definition of that word.

> **Contempt**: 1) The act of despising; lack of respect or reverence for something or someone. 2) To regard something or someone as inferior, base, or worthless; scorn. 3) The state of being despised, dishonored or disgraced. 4) Willful disobedience to a judge.

Not only does contempt show up in our attitude toward God Himself, it influences our attitude toward what He has made, including ourselves and our own bodies. Through the eyes that were opened when the first humans opted to seek after the knowledge of good and evil, we are inclined to judge that which God regarded as good. Looking at something good and regarding it as evil is eating fruit—toxic food—from the wrong tree; it is taking hold of earthly knowledge about beauty and strength and accepting it as true, rather than clinging to the truth about those things from the One who created them in us. That is what is happening when we look with envy on others, or are given impossible standards of beauty to compare ourselves to. We are comparing ourselves to a standard that God never intended for us and come away ashamed. The apostle Paul explained it this way to the church in Corinth:

> ...when they measure themselves by one another and compare themselves with one another, they are without understanding. [7]

We are not to be without understanding. We are to repent of fallen ways of thinking and, by the power of the Spirit within us, begin to challenge the shame that is the sickness that comes from eating fruit from the wrong tree.

Source of Shame

We know the source of this shame that drives our lust and gives us contempt for the body. It comes from the accuser of our brothers, the devil. Revelation 12:10 also describes him as accusing us day and night before God. The good news is that the verse prophetically states that his reign of shame is over, but the bad news is that this is yet to be fulfilled. We are still being rebuked and charged with shame, and in the world we are feeding on judgment and comparison.

The goal of the devil is to destroy unions. He wants to destroy the union between the Creator and His created. He also wants to destroy the union between husband and wife, which is a representation of the heavenly union. His strategy begins by causing a separation between the two. It is a temptation to view yourself as separate from your spouse, which destroys the image of God in the marriage.

The scheme of the devil is to draw attention to differences with criticism. To men he says: "Look: she's not as tall as others," or "she's not proportioned like that one," or "she's not as kind." Each characteristic can be compared to a mythical standard resulting in dissatisfaction. To women he says: "Look: he's not as wealthy as others," or "he doesn't work as hard as that one," or "he's not as attentive." Again, the characteristics are judged critically to fuel the temptation to be dissatisfied.

The intent of these schemes is to put a wedge between a husband and wife, eroding the value and identity of each in the eyes of the other. It can only happen along the lines of separation. The lie is that differences are bad, but God intends them to demonstrate His creativity and variety. Furthermore, those differences are what allow us to be interlocked rather than uniform.

God's way of building the union between husband and wife is that they learn intimacy together. We first see this in the creation story of Adam and Eve. As we stated before, Adam had all the living things presented before him, but no suitable partner was found. After Eve was formed, God brought her to the man. Adam looked at her and said emphatically: "Whoa, man!" and the name stuck. He had never seen anything like this, and he liked what he saw.

This is God's way for a couple, a husband and wife, to learn to create intimacy together. In His plan, the two begin in innocence. They have no other frame of reference than each other. They do not have any basis for comparisons or judgments. They are to be like Adam who, upon first seeing Eve, was astonished.

True love is a desire to know and be known. This is true intimacy that goes well beyond the physical realm and into the emotional and spiritual realms as well. Unity is demonstrated by like-mindedness, a condition where individuals are able to think alike. It is expressed by shared values, common goals, and compatible ideas. This is how two move toward oneness.

There are people that have studied the progression of relationship. According to their findings, it begins with eye contact. This signifies that each is regarding the other as a person. The next step is voice contact, whether it is a nonchalant greeting or a crafty pick-up line. This moves the relationship from the physical realm (body language) to include the emotional realm with increased communication. The relationship then progresses with physical touch along a continuum from a handshake to sexual union. This represents the connection between the two people as they merge their personalities and identities.

Intimacy, or love knowledge, follows a similar pattern using each of these communication tools. The first step of like-mindedness is to share thoughts and ideas. Everyone has thoughts and ideas, and sharing them with another carries little risk at the outset. However, these concepts transfer meaning about our core values and frame of reference which are keys to compatibility and the possibility of becoming like-minded.

The next step in melding two persons is sharing feelings and desires. Ideas, expressed as opinions, bridge the gap in progression from casual information to personal conviction. Intimacy is not possible until each person knows what the other one feels or is passionate about.

The ultimate level of intimacy is the merging of hopes and plans. This takes the relationship from the present tense to a commitment of future oneness. This is the foundation for the covenant of marriage, the binding promise that extends forward.

The problem in this world is that so few are able to begin relationships in innocence. The devil has attacked innocence with a vengeance. One of the most pervasive tools is the media. This includes entertainment through movies, television shows, the internet, as well as print media like magazines and newspapers. Its reach and influence is pervasive, with images and information that drives comparison. Famous personalities and figures are presented as a standard of perfection, where every trait is examined and criticized, compared to some mythical ideal.

This polluted paradigm of opinions and information is a loss of innocence. The images and characterizations from Hollywood introduce false standards. Soon, we compare ourselves or our spouse against that standard, and become dissatisfied with what God has created.

A little less innocuous is how innocence is lost through dirty talk. Whether it comes from uncouth comments of adolescents or immature adults, it tends to sully nakedness with shame and introduce perversity. The same is true of pornography which focuses on the physical realm, and romance novels which focuses on the emotional realm. These are tools that lead us to being judgmental and condescending toward others.

Our human nature plays into our loss of innocence as well. God created us with an appreciation and admiration for others, but we risk awakening desire before its time. Curiosity, without proper guidance and restraint, can lead to experimentation, premarital sex, and promiscuity. In cases like this, innocence is lost to another person and happens by being careless with God's precious gift of innocence.

Another way innocence is lost is through abuse. A person, at any age, can be controlled against their free will by the power or will of another. Sexual abuse is rampant, and is a particularly egregious violation of innocence. Though the person has done nothing to deserve it, they experience all the ramifications of the loss.

Innocence can also be despised. If a person does not value or care about their innocence, it is quickly lost. A primary example of this is infidelity. The thought process might be: "I need to get my needs met and have judged my spouse as insufficient to meet those needs." Infidelity can be physical, emotional or spiritual. It destroys the innocence that had been created between a husband and wife.

Loss of innocence leads to problems with intimacy. The relationship between two people should grow in closeness and operate in full disclosure. This is key to the growth of love: to know and to be known. Without this intimacy the individuals find ways to hide parts or all of themselves from each other. This is counterproductive to building oneness.

Hiding Strategies

Hiding means that I want to separate all or parts of me from all or parts of you.

Shame and lack of intimacy drive us to hide from others, just as Adam and Eve did after they sinned in the Garden of Eden. Our cover-up strategies play right into the separation of identities that the devil uses to break unions. In our classes, we use a sheet of paper cut out in the form of a leaf to remind us that hiding strategies are used to cover things up. As you learn about ways people hide, make a note which strategies you are most likely to employ and what your spouse generally turns to. This is not designed as a way to cast blame on someone, but to identify something that gets in the way of intimacy and oneness that can be addressed.

Imagine for a minute that there is an issue or topic that threatens to separate you from your spouse, and the only way to resolve it is to talk openly about it. If that scenario feels threatening to you, consider what your natural response would be. What ways might you try to avoid the conversation?

First, is *deception*. It is the first hiding strategy a person learns, and it comes as a temptation from the father of lies. You know what a lie is; it is to speak what is not true or to bear false witness. It is a sin. Aside from an outright lie, lying includes some lesser lies that seem more socially acceptable, like fibs, prevarications, or untruths. Anything that is used to deceive another person falls under the category of lies. This includes speaking words that are true, but with intent to mislead. It is a hiding strategy used to separate all or part of me from you.

Deception includes *masking, minimizing* and *avoidance*. These tools are often used by people that are deceiving themselves, as much as others. *Masking* is to put up a façade, perhaps by recharacterizing the issue. When a vulnerability is at risk of exposure, the masker offers a similar topic or issue that is less threatening to avoid the real issue.

Minimizing is used to play down the importance of an issue. Some phrases typical with minimizing are: "it's not that bad," "everyone does it," "it couldn't be helped," "I can control it," "it'll never happen again," or "you're overreacting." This is not an exhaustive list, but a fair sampling of minimizing techniques.

Avoidance is often used as a hiding strategy, and can become an elaborately choreographed dance. Hiding is sometimes physical: stepping out of the room or staying in the workshop to avoid conversation, for instance. I remember working overtime, but my motives were as much about avoidance as being magnanimous. Avoidance can also be verbal: joking, sarcasm, or changing the subject are examples. A person can become quite adept at deflecting and redirecting with a parry or thrust of skilled word play.

Passions can also be used as hiding strategies. We have heard from men and women that they "just aren't that passionate." In almost every case it is not that they are passionless, but that their passions are misplaced. For instance, a man may be passionate about his work, job, or career, so he pours himself into that and leaves nothing left to engage with his wife. This is no longer a male dominated issue, however. As a hiding strategy it comes across as: "I'm doing an important thing, and I cannot take time to be open with you."

Child raising is incredibly important, but it can be used as a hiding strategy also. The person that pours their life and soul into child rearing may leave nothing for the spouse. When the children are raised, the focus can shift to grandchildren to keep the hiding strategy viable.

When we teach about this in churches we have to illuminate a related hiding technique: volunteerism. It happens in more settings than the church, but it seems like hiding behind something as holy and ordained as ministry to God trumps any need to be honest and open with a spouse.

Three other examples come to mind, each of which is a way to hide by diverting attention: hobbies, entertainment, and other relationships. The message is that I'm too busy golfing, fishing, gardening, or whatever to have a deep and meaningful conversation with you. Entertainment is the ultimate distraction: "Can we talk about this later, after the game?" Other couples use the television as a constant distraction in the kitchen, dining room and bedroom.

We explored the directive in the first chapter that we should leave our father and mother to be joined to our wife. Sometimes other relationships, such as a family of origin, can be a hiding strategy. Similarly, a reliance on friends for encouragement, affirmation, and comfort that should be from our spouse can become a way of hiding. In these cases, we use others as a sounding board, sometimes to marshal support, instead of working out the challenges with the one to whom we are united.

Another hiding strategy that seems more prevalent in men than women, but not exclusively, is compartmentalization. It is a way in which one person is not committed at the "all in" level with their spouse. If there are unsafe topics or zones, they are placed in compartments that are held back.

Compartmentalization is often accompanied with fake vulnerability. This is a strategy where one person offers certain parts of their life or identity to scrutiny in an attempt to appear open, while at the same time guarding other compartments from exposure. It is as if they are inviting their spouse to go into any room in the house, except this closet – this topic.

Health is sometimes used as a hiding strategy. There is a cliché along this line that has been fodder for humorists and comedians for years: "Not tonight dear; I have a headache." Other health issues can be used as a dodge, such as a sleep disorder, attention deficit, depression, chronic pain, and the like. This is not to imply that health issues are psychosomatic, but very physical and very real. The point here is to identify any health issues that have become a dodge for intimacy or to cover vulnerabilities.

People hide through substance abuse. Some obvious examples are drugs and alcohol which impair a person's ability to engage. Slightly less obvious is the use of prescription drugs or other products to similar effect. Even food can be used as a barrier between a person and their spouse.

Finally, there are many ways interpersonal conflict is used to hide. When a couple gets to know each other, one of the things they learn is which buttons to push. More than that, they also learn the firing sequence. This becomes an effective hiding strategy; as soon as the topic approaches the danger zone the timid partner sets the other off, averting exposure.

A similar method is to invoke the "greater fear strategy." In this case, the hiding partner escalates the conversation. It begins as a simple inquiry with hints toward the sensitive area, and in a few volleys it gets increasingly confrontational until an explosion of conflict destroys any expectation of further communication. This is similar to the preemptive strike response, where a good defense is built around a good offense. Rather than be open, the hiding one turns the attack toward the other.

In all of these hiding strategies, and others not mentioned, the goal is to separate part or all of me from part or all of you. It maintains a chasm between two people, motivated from shame or fear, and oneness is thwarted.

Replacing Shame

Living with shame feels natural to us. We've practiced shaming and being ashamed all our lives. That's true of the whole human race, so it seems pretty normal. The good news is that God has given us the ability to learn a new way, the way that was to have been natural at the beginning. God wants us to step into a "new normal." The best place to learn the new normal, and practice it until it becomes natural is in the covenant of marriage.

In Paul's first letter to the Corinthians, he makes a big point of the interdependence that is to characterize the body of Christ, the church. He compares the church to a body and points out that each part of the body is essential for it to be a whole, functioning unit.[8] As we consider Paul's teaching on the subject, it's easy to assume that he's talking about a large group. Let's not forget, though, that the smallest functioning unit within the church is a unit made up of only two parts. That unit is called a marriage.

It is in marriage where we are to lay aside the shame that characterizes our fallen world and take up something else. That "something else" is respect. It is the recognition of a husband and wife that they are both essential parts of the body. Respect in marriage is the acknowledgement that the other party in the covenant plays a vital role in the relationship. It eagerly admits that what the other brings to the relationship is valuable. Respect must exclude two conditions: independence and dependence.

Independence is often a highly valued quality in society. It suggests self-reliance and power. In a marriage, however, it communicates two things that are very bad. Independence says, "I don't need you. I can get along quite nicely on my own." Moreover, it says, "you have no value. You are nothing." Dependence is just as bad, but for different reasons. It says, "I must need you, because I have no value."

In order for respect to replace shame in a marriage, the operative quality must be "interdependence." This quality says, "We respect one another. Because we are together, we are strengthened and have become more than the sum or our parts." In that kind of relationship each party recognizes that the other has different gifts that make him or her stronger; it recognizes that each has an important role to play that can't be exercised by one alone. As we often say, "if both of us were the same, then one of us is unnecessary!" In a godly marriage both are necessary. Both have qualities that reflect the beauty and strength of God. And that is definitely nothing to be ashamed of!

When this condition is active in a marriage we say that there exists, "mutuality." It is reciprocal respect—a two-way relationship. Mutual respect is the key to intimacy.

For mutuality to exist there needs to be a degree of maturity expressed by the parties in the relationship. In a book entitled, *Living from the Heart Jesus Gave You,*[9] the authors suggest that there are stages of development that people pass through as they go through life. We observe normal people moving from infancy through childhood and then into adulthood, parenthood (a sacrificial role) and ultimately to being what might be called an "elder," a person who is able to mentor others. Unfortunately, not all people successfully navigate through those stages by the time they look like a "grown-up."

Some people grow to a stage we might called "an infant/adult." A baby only knows one thing: what it wants and when it wants it, which is usually NOW! A baby is unable to get what it wants except by others. Infant/adults tend to rely on others to meet their needs and seem mostly unaware that people around them have needs of their own. Such a person expects the world to provide for them—"they think the world revolves around them" is a popular way to put it.

As people grow, they enter childhood, becoming somewhat self-reliant, and doing more things without help. An adult who hasn't grown past that stage could be called a "child/adult." Such a person knows how to get what he wants for himself, but like a child, doesn't seem to have the ability to be much help to others, and worse, doesn't seem very bothered by that.

An adult has learned how to not only provide for themselves, but also take care of others. Two such people, when they enter into a relationship are able to demonstrate mutual respect for one another and can strive to meet one another's needs. That is mutuality. Without it, the relationship is challenged as one, or both of the parties struggle to keep from feeling used or unsatisfied. With it, the relationship is strengthened and both husband and wife grow toward being Kingdom servants.

Intimacy in the Marriage Relationship

We have been covering intimacy issues in marriage because it is such a glaring way to show when a husband and wife are not being one flesh. It is God's original design, as evidenced by the creation of Eve. God did not make her from the ground, but from Adam's rib. As a couple, they were created from one flesh to be one flesh.

There is hope for marriages, even when there has been a long term issue about hiding and separating. Intimacy can be restored by design, even if you have never experienced it. We highlighted the divisions and their strategies not to find someone to blame, but so we could identify the area that needs to be healed. God has provided a remedy.

As we have been teaching, true love is the deep desire to know another person and to be known by them. This is the attraction of love, and the compelling aspect that allows love to grow forever.

Where there is shame in our identity, our self (ego) wants to keep it hidden. We try to protect that part and keep it from being discovered. This is driven by fear, particularly the fear that our partner will withhold love if they know the truth. This is the antithesis to oneness.

The fourth chapter of Genesis records that Adam "knew" his wife and she bore a son they named Cain. Some modern translations render it as Adam lay with his wife so there is no confusion that this refers to a sexual union. The Hebrew word is yada and literally means to know, especially to know intimately. It demonstrates the close relationship between loving in the emotional and physical realms and how each is a representation of intimacy.

In the first chapter of this book we explained that unity, or oneness, is not something that we achieve. It is a gift of God that He gives when we get married. It is something that we receive. If it has been lost, or has never been implemented in the first place, then the gift must be redeemed. That is the only way oneness, and intimacy, can be restored.

Adam and Eve were naked and unashamed because they had no shame before sin entered into the picture. A husband and wife can be restored to a no-sin condition through forgiveness. When that happens, they are able to experience oneness, without barriers or separations, in all three realms: spiritual, emotional and physical. Unity in the spiritual realm will manifest in the physical realm, and unity in the emotional realm will be evident in the spiritual realm. Like the Trinity, each of the realms are distinct and distinguishable but inseparable from the others.

My extended family has a pre-marriage tradition. On the night before the wedding there is a very special bachelor's and bachelorette's party. All the men of the family get together with the groom. Beginning with the eldest, a word of advice or encouragement is given and then a blessing is placed on him. In a separate meeting, the women do the same for the bride.

It was in this setting that my mother gave my wife invaluable advice on the night before we got married. She told her that when a husband and wife pray together it is the best aphrodisiac. That encouragement came as a shock back then, but the truth has never been forgotten.

When we minister to people with healing prayer, we often ask if they pray with their spouse. Except for perfunctory routines and reciting the Lord's prayer, the answer is usually no. That is because truly praying together is more intimate than sex.

What does it look like to be *naked and unashamed spiritually*? It begins with praying together. Part of prayer is intercession, which is the act of going to the Lord in prayer on behalf of another person. When you intercede for your spouse, you automatically seek God's will for their life. This is a unifying act. When a husband seeks God's will for his wife it matches her desires perfectly, and vice versa.

When two or more people pray they come into agreement with each other. The best solution to a difference of opinion is to pray about it together with humble hearts. God will bring you into agreement over the issue. This is the power of working it out amongst yourselves. When you have this kind of unity, being naked and unashamed is natural.

God gives us a promise to claim when we pray in unity: unhindered spiritual growth. Without this you may be double-minded and tossed about, but praying and listening together restores the Designer's unity. When the barriers and hiding strategies are put aside, a couple can be merged in their identity at the spiritual level.

What does it look like to be *naked and unashamed emotionally*? There is a confidence and trust in the other such that any emotional expression is safe. Emotions are neither good nor bad, they are an outcome of what a person believes and has experienced. For this reason, emotions are like a spotlight that shines on a person's character and frame of reference.

Barriers of fear and inhibition tend to stifle emotions. This can come from the current relationship, or can be a carryover from previous relationships. Often a person that stuffs their emotions comes from a place where it was unsafe to express them. A marriage must be a safe place for emotional expression. Sometimes it comes from self-centeredness or self-protection, and other times it comes from shame or guilt. These barriers are overcome by creating a safe environment and then practicing the expression of emotion.

It is important to share emotions so a husband and wife can learn to care the same about things. It is easy to care about the same things, but to care *the same* about them is unifying. The first practice of this is when a husband and wife care about each other, and express it. The variety of things cared about can grow from that foundation.

We act as an emotional mirror for each other. Sometimes we don't know how we feel about something until we begin to share it. My wife is very much this way, especially when she is upset about something. She tells me that she is upset, and the full extent of the emotion builds as she describes it. Often she will remark that she didn't know how bothered she was until she told me about it. This is a healthy way to process emotions. Even inappropriate emotions can be expressed in this environment, and upon scrutiny be abandoned. You owe it to your spouse to mirror back their emotions so they can get a clear understanding. Good emotions are reflected and expand. Harmful emotions are reflected and eliminated.

What does it look like to be *naked and unashamed physically*? As we said at the beginning of this chapter, there is not a shortage of nakedness in our culture, but there is a shortage of innocence. When a couple has regained their innocence they are able to be physically naked together without shame or embarrassment. For instance, an infant or toddler has no compunction about being nude because there has never been any shame associated with it.

There is no judgment in innocence because there are no competing standards. A husband finds his wife to be perfectly acceptable and pleasing because of who she is. He does not compare her form or character with any other so there is no basis for criticism or dissatisfaction. A woman finds her husband to be perfectly acceptable and pleasing in that same innocence.

God created man and woman with physical differences, and He created them with an appreciation for those differences as well. The Bible promises that a husband will be blessed by his wife and satisfied with her always when his love for her is established in godliness. The wife will be happy and satisfied with her husband always, in like fashion.

Nakedness in a marriage is one of the best tools to determine the health of a relationship. Feelings of embarrassment or immodesty should be interrogated to see if their basis is from what you believe about yourself or what you believe about your spouse. Innocence is restored by renewing your mind and becoming free from external standards.

Marital intimacy demonstrates that two people are merging into one, and at the same time it contributes to the process. The result is unity, or oneness.

As we said earlier, the gift of oneness is given by God to a husband and wife. God declares that they will become one flesh (Genesis 2). We know this to be a prophetic statement because Adam didn't have a father or mother to leave; the promise applies to us.

The prototype for this oneness is modeled in the Trinity, because the Lord God (Father, Son and Holy Spirit) is One. The marriage covenant is a replication of this model.

We need to get this oneness concept worked out in our marriages, because our marriage is the prototype for the church. Jesus prayed that we would come together in unity, as He and the Father are one. We must model this unity so the world will know that oneness is possible and that it brings glory to God. We learn to be the bride of Christ (the church) by understanding what it means to be a bride in our marriage.

Homework Assignments

1. Discuss and agree on how to create a safe environment.
2. Share five things your spouse doesn't know about you.
3. What is the greatest source of fear in your marriage? (It may not be the same for each of you.)
4. What part of your identity do you protect from others, including your spouse?
5. Write on your leaf any hiding strategies brought to your mind by the Holy Spirit. Confess them to God and then share with your spouse in a safe environment.

Marriage Rx

Chapter 4

Forgiven, Forgiving and Reconciliation

Intentional Forgiveness

In the live Marriage Rx presentations we use a video clip to remind us all that marriage is like a dance. Unless each partner is paying attention to where the other is, there is bound to be a collision or an embarrassing distance between them. The video depicts a young couple who is trying to learn the communication dance. The husband is heading out for a day of golf. His clubs are slung over his shoulder and he stops at the door to wave goodbye to his wife who doesn't seem too happy about being left alone on this sunny Saturday morning. He tries to improve the situation with a tentative, "I love you..."

Her: "OK"

Him: "You have a great day, now."

Her: "Uh-huh..."

He decides to state the obvious: "You're mad."

She does her best imitation of a wife who is not mad: "I'm not mad."

He looks puzzled. "You're not?"

She assures him she's not mad, but anyone with a splinter of perception can see that if this young man plays golf today, there will be a full blown domestic incident waiting for him when he returns. He may birdie every hole on the course, but when he comes home he will find himself seriously "in the rough."

This couple is approaching an opportunity to practice two of the most useful arts of married life: forgiveness and reconciliation.

Restored Relationships

It is a great privilege to lead someone through the steps of forgiveness, and then to see the affect it has on them. In many cases they describe a great weight being lifted off their shoulders. In other cases they remark about peace and contentment filling them up from the inside.

Forgiveness has a major impact on a person's health physically, emotionally and spiritually. Receiving forgiveness opens the door to spiritual maturity and the abundant life Jesus promises. Extending forgiveness increases our capacity to receive from God.

The need for forgiveness comes from offenses that are taken up and cause separation in relationships. Sin leads to these offenses, because to sin is to miss the mark and act in a way that is against God's design, against His will, and against His character. The first example of broken relationship comes immediately following the original sin when Adam and Eve hide, or separate themselves, from God. All separation causes pain and destroys relationship.

Sin has its damaging effect on all that are touched by it. Our sense of justice recognizes that there are consequences to sin, and there is a sense of rightness when the one that commits the sin receives some sort of punishment. But we are affected by sins committed against us, just as we are for sins committed by us. It doesn't seem fair that someone else chooses to do wrong and an otherwise innocent person suffers along with them, but that is how it works.

Sinful choices come out of rebellion or woundedness. Addictive behavior is often an attempt at self comfort because of pain in our life. The pain may be a consequence of our sin, or it may be the result of a sin committed against us. No matter where it originates, we must start with our own need to be forgiven.

Jesus taught this principle in His discourse to the Pharisees in Luke 7:40-47. The concern was pointed toward the sinful woman that had anointed the feet of Jesus and wiped them with her hair. Jesus used her example to explain that the person forgiven for much is able to love much.

Forgiveness is a gift. We receive it from God because we are all sinners in need of forgiveness.[1] The amazing truth is that the price was paid for all sinners, while they were sinners[2], and not because of anything they had done to warrant it. We all suffer pain because of separation from God, and our sinfulness causes us pain in all our relationships.

God is holding forgiveness out toward us, with extended hand, so we can accept it. The full price of sin has already been paid. It is our choice to accept it.

Steps to Being Forgiven

Forgiveness is a spiritual transaction between me and God. It is an exchange that atones for sin. Specifically, it is a trade of our guilt and consequences for Jesus' righteousness. The moment we accept the reality of forgiveness, the power of sin to separate us from God is cancelled. Our relationship is restored at once.

1. Conviction

Conviction means to become aware of sin. It is the role of the Holy Spirit to convict men of sin[3], and the role of man to be sensitive to that conviction. Our conscience is not the same as the Holy Spirit, though an innocent conscience will work like the Spirit. We must work to maintain a good conscience, because if our conscience becomes seared it is no longer an accurate measure of right and wrong.

Conviction triggers an emotional response, but it does not leave us with feelings of guilt or shame. Those come from the devil, the accuser of the brethren[4] that wants only to separate unions and destroy relationships. No matter how much guilt you carry, it cannot atone for sin. Sin must be forgiven.

Pay attention to the specific emotion experienced when the Holy Spirit convicts of sin. It may be embarrassment, sadness, disappointment in self, or frustration. When we feel that way, it is the Spirit's way of making us aware of the thing that is separating us from Him. He does that for one purpose: so we can be restored into oneness with God.

Be aware that the Holy Spirit may involve our spouse in bringing a sin to our attention. It is the role of the one-flesh partner to act as a mirror to reveal things that would otherwise be hidden from the other. Learn to be sensitive to the feeling of conviction rather than be hardened by it. It is the first step toward being forgiven.

2. Confess

When we are confronted with our sin, we must go to God and confess that sin. The most important part of confessing is to take an account. Jesus taught about this in the parable of the unforgiving servant.[5] The story opens with the master taking account of his affairs, doing an assessment of what is owed and who is responsible for the debt. When conviction brings sin to our attention, the next step is to accurately determine its nature and scope. We need to be regularly taking an account and recognize the full extent of what we owe.

No one likes to be guilty of sin, so the natural man tries to deny it. Of course, once conviction has set in, denial requires lying and so compounds the sin. The outright lie is one form of denial, but another form is to ignore the conviction. Some people go to great lengths to distract themselves from ever asking the question of right or wrong in a matter.

Another barrier to confession is when we try to justify ourselves. God will let us try, but only He can truly justify. We can catch ourselves trying to justify by listening to what we say after "but."

"...but I was trying to do the right thing. My motives were pure."

"...but it isn't any worse than what everyone else does."

"...but I was tricked into it (or forced into it)."

Don't minimize sin, either. Take an accurate accounting because we can't get more forgiveness than we ask for. Minimizing sin is when we downplay the seriousness of the offense in an attempt to reduce its sinfulness. Some examples of minimizing are:

"... nobody was hurt by it."

"... I was not entirely honest (instead of confessing a lie)."

For example, imagine that I owe a friend a hundred thousand dollars. This makes me uncomfortable around him, so I humble myself to ask for mercy, confessing that I owe a great deal of money and cannot repay. If I timidly admit to only forty thousand dollars, I may be granted mercy and still owe sixty thousand. When asking for mercy we should admit the full extent of the debt and receive as much grace as is available.

Confess the offense of the sin, not the event. The offense is the debt that is owed to another, whereas the event is the occasion in which the debt was incurred. When a person forgives it makes a change in what is owed even though it cannot change the historical event.

Let me illustrate with a story. A young boy noticed warm chocolate chip cookies on the counter in the kitchen. It was mid-afternoon and no one was around. He knew mom would make him wait until after dinner if he asked for a cookie now, so he swiped one quickly "and he did eat."[6] Now this is not an egregious sin, but his loving mother would wish to bring conviction to him none the less.

In this simple example, the sin event was stealing the cookie. This was not the primary offense because the wrong could be made right if the boy either replaced the cookie or exchanged it for something of equal value. Even if he were able to do that, the offense of the sin would still be outstanding. The child owes his mom honor, respect and obedience, so that is the unpaid debt from the offense of disobedience and dishonor.

If the child admitted taking the cookie, it is reasonable that his mom would forgive him. The cookie is not of great consequence and costs mom very little in time and material. However, the offense of disobedience and dishonor would still be outstanding. These are the greater offenses that need to be confessed.

We have a promise from God that when we confess our sins to Him, He will certainly forgive us.[7] Being forgiven requires that we confess the sin to whomever we owe it, to the one that has taken the offense or has the right to do so. King David modeled how we should confess our sin to God and to others.[8] It is easier to confess to God with the promise that He will forgive, compared to confessing to another person who might withhold forgiveness.

3. Ask for Mercy

We have a moral obligation to repay our debts if we are able to do so. However, if we do not have the means to repay then all we can do is to ask for mercy. This requires a humble attitude on the part of the sinner. We must surrender all our rights to the outcome, that is the disposition of the debt, and submit entirely to the will of the one holding the offense.

God promises to forgive us every time we confess our sin to Him and ask for mercy. We can trust Him to cancel the debt and its power to separate us from Him. This is not necessarily the case with others. They hold all rights to the debt and can choose to release us from it, or continue to hold us accountable. King David confessed confidently before God, knowing that being forgiven by Him was the most important thing. We should do the same.

Forgiveness is a free gift from the one who shows mercy and must be offered with no strings attached. Anything less is an exchange or trade, and not true forgiveness. Any condition placed on the debtor is an attempt to extract value in place of the debt owed.

"I'll forgive you as long as you never do that again!" This is a common statement, but not true forgiveness. It is an example of trading the debt for a promise, and a promise with a track record of being broken, besides.

"I'll forgive you for that, but from now on you'd better be extra nice to me." This is a variation of the previous condition. It is an exchange of a current debt for future favor.

When asking for mercy, the debtor is requesting that the offense be released, not that history be rewritten. In the stolen cookie scenario, imagine that the boy was convicted by his mom about taking the cookie. She might ask: "Did you take a cookie without permission?"

The boy might quickly reply: "Yes mom, and I'm sorry I took it. Please forgive me." This would be akin to admitting the error of the event and asking mom to forget that it happened. This is not true forgiveness. Neither the boy nor his mom can forget the event, and it certainly cannot be rewritten.

Since the offense is the debt, and the event is just the occasion in which the offense occurred, the boy should ask for mercy like this: "Yes mom, and I'm sorry I took it. Please forgive me for disobeying you and not showing you the honor and respect you deserve."

True forgiveness happens when the debtor asks for mercy and the creditor complies with the request.

4. Repent

This leads to repentance. We that have been forgiven experience a change in our condition. The debt we could not repay has been forgiven and we will never be obligated to it again. There may be a strong emotional response of relief and an accompanying realization that things are different. This new condition triggers a change in attitude, and it is kept by an act of will. Maintaining a new attitude, repentance, is an intentional choice.

But repentance does not precede forgiveness, nor is it a condition upon which forgiveness is granted. It follows as the heart of the sinner is changed and accompanies the change in our identity. The new attitude affects what we believe to be true and becomes part of our identity. Our behavior derives from that identity, and then the actions change as a result of the repentant attitude. It is automatic.

The truly repentant heart will do "deeds in keeping with repentance."[9]   Notice that these things are done in response to the change, not in payment for the debt or to extract or coerce forgiveness.

A good example of this is the instruction in Ephesians that one who steals should repent and instead work with their hands so they will have something to share.[10] The work and generosity are behaviors that demonstrate a new identity. The forgiven person is no longer a thief, but a contributor. Just like the change in attitude, the change in behavior is a result, not a payment or trade for the release from the debt.

In the process of repenting, we should ask God if there are any actions that need to be taken. Sometimes God will have specific instructions to be obeyed, and other times it may be a matter of conscience such as Zacheus' promise to repay with interest those he had cheated.

5. Release

This is a promise to claim in the process of being forgiven. God is the one that releases us sinners from what we owe. No matter how awful the offense, from God's point of view it is released. If God releases us, shouldn't we release ourselves from the debt? That is what we must do to fully accept His forgiveness and be free from the debt we owe.

6. Relationship

When God forgives us, He atones for the sin. We are made righteous and justified. From God's perspective it is just as if we had never sinned. Our identity is restored to what He, as the Designer, originally specified. This is the condition we must be in for unhindered relationship with Him.

Our destiny is what God created us to be. It is our sweet spot, when we are being exactly as God designed us to be and in perfect relationship with Him. To be forgiven means that we are restored to that destiny and have become a new creation. In fact, when we are being exactly like He designed us to be, we are perfectly acceptable to Him. We are living according to God's will and moving toward His preferable future for us. This is the eternal relationship we have with Him. That is what it means to be reconciled to God.

If we are forgiven by another person it restores the potential for relationship. Any debt owed by one person to another causes a breach in their relationship. When the debt has been paid or forgiven, then it no longer comes between them. Being forgiven opens the door to restored relationship.

Forgiveness is a Gift

Forgiveness, that is "to be forgiven," is a gift that we can receive from God. He offers the forgiveness because the price for all sin has been paid. We choose to accept His offer, or not. If we do choose to accept it, then we experience restored relationship with Him. In that reconciled relationship with Him we can express our love by offering forgiveness to others that have offended and hurt us. It is worth remembering that those who have been forgiven much also love much.[11]

In the prayer room, when we are leading people toward the steps of forgiving, the sticking point comes as they are taking an account of the debt owed to them. The pain of the offense is real, and this makes it a struggle to extend forgiveness. Mentally rehearsing how much God has forgiven us should be enough to settle the argument; nevertheless, it is hard to forgive others that have caused so much pain.

It is not helpful to use scripture as a goad. The disciples asked Jesus to teach them to pray, and in response He gave us "The Lord's Prayer." At the conclusion of it, He specifically teaches that you must forgive others.[12] Later, He taught the parable of the unforgiving servant, which concludes with a very strong admonition to forgive, or else.[13] Forgiving others is a command to obey.

Be careful, though. Taken in this context a person may be inclined to regard the command as if it were a huge burden to bear. It seems like an onerous task to find forgiveness for the one that has caused the pain. It is not possible to conjure up forgiveness, or to create it from inside. The conclusion: "I simply cannot forgive."

There is good news. One of the principles that the Kingdom of Heaven operates on is giving and receiving. We can offer forgiveness because we have received it. We did not receive forgiveness because of our worth, or that we somehow merited it, nor because we asked for it. It was a free gift that we accepted. We do not confess our sin so that we will be forgiven[14] but so we will know what we have been forgiven of. Christ died for us while we were still undeserving sinners.[15]

A number of years ago, one of my sisters made some choices that offended and caused pain to everyone in the family. It caused a huge rift and she was certainly unable to repay the debt.

"I'm ready to forgive her," I said to one of my siblings, feeling rather magnanimous, spiritual and mature because of this profession. Then I continued: "But she hasn't asked for forgiveness."

This added condition is not compatible with God's way of giving. Forgiveness is offered freely to the sinner, who only needs to accept it. Since forgiveness is offered freely, if we accept it, it frees us. When we accept it, we have it! We do not have to find it, buy it, dig it up, or earn it. It is a gift that we receive.

When we recognize that God makes it this simple to get forgiveness, then we can offer it to someone in need of forgiveness.[16] If they receive it, it will free them. It is not a burden after all. We received it as a free gift and we have the privilege of offering it to someone else.

Now we can review the command to obey about forgiveness in a new light. The promise to claim that accompanies the command is that we can receive first, and then give. Do not judge or condemn, but rather forgive. When you give forgiveness it will be given to you in increasing measure.[17] Those who have been forgiven much are able to love much, and one of the greatest gifts to give in love is forgiveness.

Steps to Forgiving

Having received forgiveness, we have the capacity to forgive others. Forgiving others requires an intentional act of our will. It is not difficult to do, but can be a hard choice to make. The steps to forgiving someone are similar to the steps we identified for being forgiven.

1. Take an Account

The first step is to make an accurate assessment of the debts owed to us and the offenses that are getting in the way of relationship. We begin taking an account by considering our relationship with our spouse. "What is separating me from him or her?" "Why am I feeling like putting distance between us?" "What gets in the way of us being one flesh?" We can continue in this vein with our family, friends, co-workers, neighbors, and others. Wherever there is broken or strained relationship, dig in to find what offenses are in play.

Ask the Holy Spirit to help identify things that must be forgiven. Just as He convicts of sin so we know where we need to be forgiven, He also convicts us of harboring bitterness, judgment or grudges against others. Our spouse can be used by the Holy Spirit to bring some of these things to mind. When that happens, thank him or her.

We need to identify the sin to release it. Forgetting or suppressing the offense is not the same as releasing it. The adage that we should "forgive and forget" is not helpful. When we deny our feelings, especially offenses that we harbor against others, the burden stays in our body. Because we are physical, emotional and spiritual beings, when we carry a burden in one area it affects us in the other areas as well. For instance, to carry an emotion of bitterness can manifest in the physical realm as distress or disease, and holding unforgiveness creates a conflict that shows up as pain and sickness.

It is appropriate to interject an observation at this point. We take an account so that we can know what is already standing between us. It is not to create a rift or to stir up something that is benign. It is not to find someone to blame. It is to discover *who* we need to forgive and specifically *what* we need to forgive.

We must identify the offense, not just the event in which it occurred. The offense is the thing we personally hold against the other person, and it doesn't matter if others agree with our assessment. We are holding them accountable for it, and that is what makes it an outstanding debt.

A fellow Christian man asked me if I would forgive him. He and I had had a falling out several years before. I asked him what he would like to be forgiven for. He began to recount some of the events surrounding our disagreement, admitted the error of some of the choices he had made, and expressed sorrow at the way things turned out. It was as if he wanted me to blot those memories from my mind so we could go on living as if they had never occurred. He did not address the offenses that had driven us apart, but implied that he wished they were not there. He was confused regarding 'forgive and forget.'

I told him that I had already forgiven him. Interestingly, he was quite offended when I outlined to him what I had forgiven. He hadn't taken an account of the offenses, nor did he want to own responsibility for the things I had held against him. When it comes to taking an account of what is owed, the forgiver is the one that defines the debt, not the debtor.

Explore the emotions and beliefs contained in the event to learn what the offenses are. Recall the event, and then consider how it makes you feel. What emotions are rising up? Emotions are a response, and they are neither good nor bad. They point to the belief to which they are anchored. When you are re-experiencing the feelings ask yourself why this emotional response is there. It will point you to what you believe the person owes.

For instance, it is a sin to commit adultery and infidelity causes great problems in a marriage. We must forgive our spouse for the offenses of the sin, not just the event. In our prayer ministry, when we have interrogated this belief there are always personal offenses that have been taken. They may include rejection, disloyalty, disrespect, selfishness, dishonesty, and a lot more. The offenses reveal what is owed: acceptance, loyalty, respect, unconditional love, honesty, and so on.

2. Acknowledge the Debt

We must admit to ourselves that we are holding the person responsible for the debt they owe us. Acknowledging the debt is an intentional step, and the more specific we are in it the more effective will be our forgiving.

There can be a tendency to minimize or suppress the offense. It hurts to remember what someone owes. It is painful to reconsider what we are doing without because of someone else's choices. It can also feel like we are losing ground by bringing these things back up. We must keep in mind that the goal is true forgiveness.

For example, a young man came to me because of father wounding. He had a harsh childhood and suffered from many sins of his father. As I led him in the process of taking an account, we hit an unexpected snag. The young man remembered the fifth commandment that says: "Honor your father and your mother that the days may be long in the land that the LORD your God is giving you." [18] He began to minimize and justify the offenses, making excuses for his father. I understood the mental conflict he was going through, but to pursue this was the path he needed to take to get to a place of forgiving.

He thought I was rather harsh when I explained what the offenses really were. God had given his father an assignment to raise him with unconditional love from a completely dependent infant to a mature and independent man with a vibrant relationship with God. He had failed in his assignment. There was a long list of things his father owed and was unable to pay. As I helped him explore these grievances, he went from being disappointed in his dad to being good and mad at him!

Be angry, yet do not sin.[19] When you acknowledge the debt owed to you it will cause an emotional response. An appropriate response to sin is anger. Allow that anger to rise up. Emotions are neither good nor bad, they are simply responses. But be angry against the sin, not against the dad. That is the difference captured in Ephesians; be angry (normal response), but do not sin (harboring bitterness against the debtor.) As the anger rises up we are getting closer to the place where the person can be forgiven.

Recognize that the offender does not have the means to repay. The offender just cannot do it. They may not have the wherewithal or they may not have the will, but they are unable to pay what they owe. We can hang onto the hope that they will repay it somehow or sometime. We can file a claim and demand payment. We can hang onto a lien, but if we do, then that is all we have. An IOU is the right to expect and demand payment, but holding onto it from someone we already know has no means to repay is either stubborn or foolish, or both.

The emotional response of anger is appropriate upon the realization of what is owed, and this is a necessary step to set up forgiveness. If we try to move too quickly past this step it leads to judgment which blocks us from forgiving. If we are unwilling to forgive because we demand payment, that is a form of judgment. However, if we are unwilling to acknowledge the debt, or stop short of feeling the anger rise up, then we move to pity. Pity is also a form of judgment because pity judges the debtor as a horrible person condemned to get what they deserve, while at the same time feeling sorry for their plight. We assess damages comparatively, believing that the person would suffer so much more were it not for our generosity. Unfortunately, for both debtor and collector, judgment (whether condemnation or pity) traps each in their condition.

3. Find Compassion

Compassion is moved by mercy and contains no judgment. In compassion I can see the world from another person's perspective rather than my own. This is what Jesus demonstrated when He chose to heal the sick and when He cried over Jerusalem. Putting Himself in their position, He understood their condition and trouble.

It takes mercy to forgive. Mercy is the act of replacing judgment with loving-kindness. God demonstrates this in how He deals with our sinfulness, and He has created us in His image. We are able to choose loving instead of exacting punishment.

It is not love to condone or approve of sin in another person's life. Love is to prefer, or want the best for, another person. Love, as a verb, is an action whereby you do something to help another person toward the preferable future God has designed for them. If you are in relationship with your spouse or family member, and they are walking in sin, the offense of that sin will interrupt relationship with you and others. Similarly, tolerance or political correctness are not loving, either. These may be borne out of extreme self-centeredness or absolute apathy, but they do not lead another toward truth and life.

We have to find compassion within us. If we allow the emotional response of anger to grow then there is a fulcrum effect that allows the compassion to rise on the other side. First, we have to see the sin for what it is and realize the damage it causes. Then we have to see the other person as a person. When we do that, we can see how the sin affects them as much as it affects us. Just as we wish to be set free from the effects of the sin, so we can see that they need the same freedom.

4. Release All Rights to the Debt

Furthermore, we must release all our rights to the repayment of that debt in the past, present and future. It is important to acknowledge that the person did not pay what they owed in the past, and that it is impossible to collect from them historically. Then it is important to release the right to collect payment from them in the present, reminding ourselves that the debtor no longer owes it to us. Finally, we are releasing all future rights to extract payment from the debtor of this debt.

It would be false forgiveness to pretend that we have released the debtor, and then secretly hope or expect them to make it good in the future. True forgiveness means to release them from the debt, completely. One of our hypothetical tests of complete forgiveness is to imagine that the debtor, who we know does not have the means to repay the debt, has a change in circumstances. How would you feel about what they owe you then?

For instance, pretend that you chose to forgive someone who borrowed several hundred dollars from you and could not repay it. Even though you really needed the money, you released them from the debt. A few weeks later you discover that they just received a substantial inheritance. If you truly released the rights to the debt, they are under no obligation to pay you despite their turn of circumstances.

Releasing the debt is a spiritual transaction, and should be confessed as true before God as our witness. It is not necessary to tell the person that has been forgiven in order for them to be released. In fact that is impossible to do when we forgive someone with whom we no longer have contact either due to death or distance. I recommend a release statement like this: "God, I confess to You that I release (insert name here) from the debt I believe they owe me, and declare that I have surrendered all rights to collect, now or ever."

This step is a choice that we enter into of our own free will. The release is a gift that costs us something, and we are willing to give it to the other person. It is not a trade or exchange.

There is a human tendency to try to extract something of value from the debtor, and it can come in subtle ways. For instance, you may trade the debt for a penitent heart, as suggested earlier by the idea of forgiving someone if they come and ask for it. It is an exchange to release the debt contingent on the person's humility. It is an exchange to forgive only in response to the person's suffering or pain. It is a trade to give release but demand a promise, which of course is probably an empty promise anyway.

The source of forgiveness is God. When we can't find it in our heart to forgive them for what they did, we must ask God to give it to us first. We may hesitate because their sin hurt too much, or it cost us too much, and then we have to choose. When this has been extremely difficult for a person, I recommend that they ask God to forgive the person. Once God has forgiven them, it is easier to do the same.

This spiritual transaction happens between us and the person in the spiritual realm, and may or may not be evident in the physical or emotional realms. It is also a transaction between us and God. Until we release the right to collect from the person, God can't give us what He wants to give us in its place.

When Jesus died on the cross, He paid for all sin. God is in the paying business, which is the meaning of atonement. When we hang onto our spouse's obligation, waiting for him or her to pay, we are unable to accept the good gift God has in mind for us. It is as if our hands are filled with an IOU that obliges the other person to pay, but also obliges us to collect only from them. When we release that, then our hands are open. The sin and debt is a real loss, but Jesus died for all of it. Now that we have let go of our right to collect from the debtor, we can receive payment from God instead.

Consider the ramifications of this truth. Maybe someone was not able to give you the honor you deserved. When you release them, God says that He will repay it for them. Maybe someone took away an opportunity from you and is unable to make good on that debt. When you release him, God says that He will repay it instead. Think of all the possibilities! We should be quick to forgive everybody, because when God pays, it is really good stuff. The alternative is an IOU from someone with a lousy track record.

I used this example to describe the need to release debts with the young man that needed to forgive his dad. I said: "You get to make a choice, like on a television show where you get to choose a door. Behind door number one is an IOU that is already in default and will never be paid. Behind door number two is God's richest blessings and good things.[20] Knowing this, which door will you choose?"

"Well, I'd have to go with door number two in that case," he chuckled.

"Good choice. The Father of Lights gives every good thing,[21] and He gives more than you can ask or imagine.[22] That's a much better choice than an empty promise that will never happen."

5. Seek Reconciliation

The forgiver is free to establish a redeemed relationship with the one forgiven because the impediment is removed. Just as sin separates us from others, forgiveness opens the door for restoration.

For instance, let's say that you borrowed some money from your parents when you were a young adult. You remember that you owe it, but never talk about it because it's not convenient to repay it with your current budget. Your parents know that you borrowed it, but they never talk about it because they don't want to make you feel bad. Even though it is never discussed, everyone knows about it and it quietly looms large, like the proverbial elephant in the living room.

One day you think that you would like to go on a vacation. Of course, you want to enjoy it, but you don't want your parents to know that you are going. Deep down you know that you could pay them back with that money, or at least make a dent in the amount you owe. They might wonder why you spent that money on your own pleasure instead of paying what you owe them. So, either you go on vacation with a guilty conscience, or you choose not to go and feel beleaguered.

Probably the thoughts outlined here are assumed, but never spoken. You guess how your parents feel about it, and they guess how you do. Notice the rift in the relationship.

Then comes Thanksgiving and you sit down with the family for dinner. It's safe to talk about the weather, and other innocuous topics, but you don't talk about vacation plans because it gets in the way of relationship. Spoken or unspoken, there is a barrier between you.

Imagine instead that you go to your parents and talk about it. You confess that you owe them money and agree with them on the amount. Then you speak honestly about your ability to repay the loan, and beg for forgiveness for any amount you do not have the means to repay. One way or another, you want to agree to an arrangement that resolves the hidden debt. When that happens, it removes the barrier to relationship. You have the ability to be reconciled.

Consequence of Sin in Relationships

There is an old saying: Time heals all wounds. In relationships, however, time can cover a wound, but may do nothing to heal it. A careless word, consistent disregard for the needs of the other or unfaithfulness can inflict injury that, if left untended, will compromise the relationship.

An injury left untreated is vulnerable to infection. Even a minor injury that becomes infected can be serious, at times fatal. In some jungle environments an open wound that is not properly cleansed and covered will become a magnet for flying insects that can deposit bacteria, even lay eggs in the wound. The resulting infection can spread throughout the body and even result in the wound healing over the infection and becoming abscessed.

In a marriage, wounds—the emotional kind—also need cleansing and covering or they, too, can cause serious damage to the relationship. The cleansing process requires forgiveness and reconciliation. Without such care a marriage is vulnerable to infections. Injury from sin, disappointment, grief, judgment can become infected with bitterness and anger, or with detachment and indifference. The initial sin that caused the injury makes us vulnerable to further sin that comes in by our reaction.

Most wounds in a relationship fall into three categories: betrayal, abandonment and rejection. The feelings that result from such wounds are often prevented from healing by deception and, sometimes, the demonic. Warfare in the spiritual dimension can gain an internal advantage by manipulating the wounded heart and using the injury to undermine relationships. Though the original wound seems to have healed—what's in the past is done, after all—the infection that remains may be slowly killing the relationship.

False healing of an emotional wound is made possible when an injured person learns to compensate for the injury. Have you ever cut a finger or injured your foot? As the injury heals, you devise ways to protect the hurt place. You get along without the damaged digit by holding it out straight instead of using it to grip the steering wheel as you would normally. Or in the case of a foot, you learn to put more weight on the uninjured leg, thus walking with a limp. Sometimes, out of habit, we continue to limp even after the wound is healed.

Similarly, we learn to compensate for unhealed emotional wounds. We call such strategies "survival skills" or "coping mechanisms." The victim of a shattered home life and unavailable nurturing parent may learn to hide the pain by developing a "sense of humor" to conceal the pain inside. A husband that feels unappreciated by his wife stays late at the office, or finds satisfaction in helping neighbors with minor household repairs rather than be at home and face his failure; a wife avoids certain subjects to keep from being belittled by her demeaning spouse. We adopt survival skills while living with long term or untreated trauma. Sometimes the patterns persist after the initial trauma has passed, often going unrecognized by the one caught in them. Emotionally, we walk with a "limp."

This is why the tools of forgiveness need to be used skillfully in our relationships. If we neglect to seek forgiveness or refuse to practice it, we invite sin to take advantage of the injury and make a place for harmful coping strategies that divide and damage our marriage.

Ongoing Forgiveness

One of the tricky things about forgiveness is that it is often not a one-time event, but an intentional and consistent choice.

A number of years ago, we (Dan and Jody) had a painful church experience. Long-term friendships seemed to morph into adversarial relationships over a period of weeks. In the end, the "friends" became accusers and ended the relationship, leaving us confused and deeply hurt. Things were said that we never imagined we would hear from our friends. In the aftermath of one particularly painful meeting, we determined that we would leave the ministry. Our conclusion was that if these things were true of us we had no business trying to work in the name of the Lord. Clearly, we were disqualified.

The experience helped us understand the depth of what the Psalmist wrote. There is nothing like personal experience to underscore the deep emotion contained in his words:

> Indeed, it is not an enemy who insults me, or else I could bear it; It is not one who hates me who arrogantly taunts me, or else I could hide from him. But it is you, a man like me, my close friend in whom I confided. We would share personal thoughts with each other...[23]

Ultimately, we did not give up. We kept doing what we felt called to do, but the healing process took literally years. It was no simple matter to regain our confidence and to move beyond that hurtful time, to trust that we weren't disqualified by some destructive flaws that were hidden from us.

The process of healing required forgiveness, not just a glib "let bygones be bygones" utterance, but a process of forgiveness over the years of healing. Consider, for a moment, Jesus' words to His disciples in Matthew 18.

> Then Peter came to him and said, "Lord, how many times must I forgive my brother who sins against me? As many as seven times?" Jesus said to him, "Not seven times, I tell you, but seventy times seven! [24]

We used to understand this verse as a command to forgive each time someone did something wrong to you, even if he kept doing things to you after you forgave. But our experience—over the years we've come to call it our "Kaaboom"—taught us that sometimes forgiveness is a process, even a discipline. It feels like it must "flow up hill." In the months after the "kaaboom," we often found our thoughts returning to the experience—echoes of the original offenses—remembering things that had been said and done. Every recollection would reawaken the hurt, causing us to sense again the painful feelings. To allow that to continue—to dwell on those feelings—is the classic definition of resentment: to "re-sense" a past incident.

Forgiveness, we discovered, required us to utter a prayer of forgiveness every time one of those past events would elbow its way into our thoughts. In essence, we learned that to forgive someone up to "seventy times seven" may mean that we are to be ready to forgive the same event regardless of how often it comes to mind. We were to let each memory, no matter how many times it recurred, be a trigger for thanksgiving.

The end result was that the memories came back less and less frequently and when they did, the resentment began to fade. Eventually, those wounds became powerless to inflict pain. They had been exploited by the demonic, used to keep the hurt fresh and to distract us from the important work that God had for us, but forgiveness healed the wounds, and in a few cases, led to reconciliation.

A word about reconciliation. Another thing we learned from the "kaaboom" is that it is not possible to reconcile with those who insist on holding you under their judgment. Conversely, if you insist on holding others under your judgment, you will have effectively erected a barrier that will prevent you from walking with the one you judge. Reconciliation requires both forgiveness and willingness to trust the work of God in the other; to acknowledge that we (and that includes the one with whom you wish to reconcile) are all under construction and that God can be trusted with the work. Unless both parties in a broken relationship can learn to walk in that confidence, reconciliation will be impossible.

Paul, the apostle put it in his letter to the Romans:

> Live in harmony with one another. Do not be haughty, but associate with the lowly. Never be conceited. Repay no one evil for evil, but give thought to do what is honorable in the sight of all.

If possible, so far as it depends on you, live peaceably with all. (vs. 12:16-18 ESV, italics mine).

As much as we might like to reconcile with someone, even a spouse, it isn't completely up to us. Once we have done what we can to forgive and to invite relationship, a restored friendship will require the putting away of judgment.

Reconciliation

The goal of forgiveness is reconciliation. As the scripture says: "So far as it depends on you, live in peace with all people." [25] That is why we do the spiritual transaction before God that releases another from the debt they owe us and allows God to make it right. In similar fashion, we need to be reconciled with each other, just like we are being reconciled with God. To be reconciled means to be one flesh and one spirit together, with our fellow man and with God.

Sin separates identities. It divides the oneness by forcing distinctions and focusing on them. Comparison and judgment identifies me as me, and you as you. It declares that this part of you is not me, and this part of me is not you, dividing one from the other rather than merging them. This leads to hiding strategies, self-centeredness or silo mentalities. Then the self-identification causes one to withdraw and another to attack.

Instead we want to be reconciled. Then the differences go away or are appreciated. We discover that we have things in common or that complement each other. Our relationship can grow and develop together; it can merge.

Reconciliation in relationships is when the union between individuals is restored to God's design. It's not just making nice. It's not just being socially acceptable when in the public eye. It's not a matter of each controlling his behavior in a way that hides the conflict. It is only reconciliation when the relationships are united according to God's plan.

We noticed this in our children as they grew up. In the years from elementary school through high school there would be occasions where sin would cause a separation between them. It could happen between any two of them, because we had three. The arguments and conflict seemed to them to be irreconcilable differences. Each would stand in opposition to the other with anger and accusation, blaming the other and trying to protect their rights.

"Okay, the two of you come into the living room and sit on the couch." As soon as they complied, we continued: "You will sit here together, holding hands, until you are able to get along with each other."

At first they would be holding to their rights and positions, the same ones that were driving them apart, and they would glare at each other full of anger and self-righteousness. Pretty soon their tempers would calm, and they would be able to sit civilly together. Perhaps they would agree that the discipline was worse than the offenses they held against the other. Before long they would be talking and chuckling, building some camaraderie against a common foe. Reconciliation took shape as they realized all they had in common compared to the pettiness of their differences.

Differences can happen in grownups, too. When two adults take opposing positions it can cause conflict in their relationship. We tell them that they have to be reconciled, so they put on an act around each other. This can even happen at church. Though they have not mended their relationship, they are nice to each other publicly, appearing to be reconciled. Reconciliation is more than acting in socially acceptable ways, such as smiling when appropriate or saying pleasant things to someone's face. Not that being socially acceptable or polite is a bad thing! In fact, it is quite good. But it is not reconciliation.

Neither is it reconciliation to condone or tolerate a sinful identity. Overlooking sin, ignoring or suppressing it does not promote truth, healing or unity. The sin has to be forgiven to be reconciled.

Reconciliation is loving one another. Jesus explains the great commandment to love one another in John 15 to show what real love looks like.[26] It is not very often that someone will give up their life for another, though that is the measure of love. So to be reconciled we must love, and to love we must be willing to give something up for the other person.

Let's be practical: Husbands, are you willing to give up your life for your wife? Wives, are you willing to give up your life for your husband? Sometimes we're not even willing to give up our opinion! Sometimes we're not willing to give up our hobby, our free time, or our leverage, let alone give up our life. But true reconciliation is this: saying I am willing to give up my right to myself in exchange for the promise of being one flesh.

Then the things that come between us will prompt us to make a spiritual transaction and forgive. We will give up what is owed and let God make good on it instead. Then our relationship can be restored, and we can be reconciled into that one flesh and one spirit relationship. It means that my identity and your identity will merge.

The picture is not just husbands and wives, though that's significant. The picture is a very physical representation of what happens in the spiritual realm when God forgives us and His identity is merged with ours. God forgives us and reconciles us; He removes the barriers so that we can merge identities with Him! We become one spirit with Him. This is a great mystery, but we'll have all eternity to figure it out.

We're seeing it played out in the family, between husbands and wives, but it is even bigger than that.

In the unreconciled home, identities are separated because of sin. Sin is an attack on identity because the devil desires to destroy the works of God. We are created in His image, but sin mars the reflection. The presence of sin causes us to focus on the differences between us, assuming that all differences are incompatibilities. Our response is to move to judgment and comparison which are fruit of the Tree of Knowledge of Good and Evil.

Adam and Eve were completely unselfconscious in front of each other before sin entered the Garden of Eden. They did not judge or compare one another. Instead they appreciated seeing in the other just what God wanted them to see. They were a perfect complement one to the other, and they had been created specifically for that purpose. They were naked and unashamed.

As soon as sin entered into the relationship their perspective changed. Shame was introduced. The sin clouded their vision and they no longer saw what they appreciated about each other; instead they saw things they judged and found offensive in one another. Sin caused a wedge to come between them that separated their identities. The tool that drives the wedge is blame. The separated and isolated identity seeks to protect itself by casting blame and placing responsibility on anyone outside of self. This is an attempt to get out of sin by passing it around instead of eradicating it. But we are changed from sin to righteousness through forgiveness.

One of the challenges to transformation is what we call "persistence of identity." When our sin nature has been our identity, we may hold to some old patterns and ways of thinking. Instead of being transformed by the renewing of our mind[27] we revert back to the habits and beliefs that held us in our sinful nature. The old identity tries to persist, resisting the change that comes from God to heal us. It can be an internal or environmental issue.

We see this happen in our prayer ministry. When a person is set free by the truth of God and the love of Jesus, they return to their home where relationships have not changed. Their change is viewed as uncomfortable, and the unchanged spouse or family demands that the person return to their former identity. For example, a wife that has been in a victim role for many years receives healing from Jesus and experiences freedom. Her husband and family are not pre-pared to relate with her in that freedom and demand that she revert to the role of victim. We use the example of family life, but the same is true in all relationships, such as extended family, work, community, school or church.

This is one of the reasons it is so important for a husband and wife to follow the instructions to leave their father and mother to be joined to their spouse.[28] The pressure and in-fluence can be very insidious as the familiar but harmful ways are protected. We must leave an environment that would confine us to old identities.

Persistence of identity works to the advantage of the couple that grows together and is being transformed by the renewing of their minds. As each receives truth, they are able to confirm the transformation and mutually encourage mind renewal rather than be trapped in an old paradigm.

The Apostle Paul has given us some great insight for reconciliation in his second epistle to the Corinthians. He says "From now on, therefore, we regard no one according to the flesh."[29] That means he is not considering them from a worldly point of view, nor judging them according to the Old Covenant. To do so is to measure a person by their failure. In order to be reconciled, we must be willing to give away the

Old Covenant assessment. In its place we receive reconciliation with God through Christ.

"If anyone is in Christ, he is a new creation. The old has passed away, behold, the new has come." [30] We are a new creation as a result of being forgiven. That means we have a new identity. It is the new identity that peels away the old and sinful parts and allows us to look like God designed us to look. It is our sweet spot, our destiny, to be the person that God had in mind when He first conceived of us, and long before we were conceived in the natural realm. It is His preferable future for each of us: righteousness.

If we, as a husband and wife, are trying to be reconciled with each other then we must each have our identity reconciled with God.

When God reconciles us to Himself, He makes us a new creation. It changes our identity. If the two of us are trying to be reconciled with each other, but my identity is out of balance with who I'm supposed to be, then there isn't a proper identity for her to reconcile with. In fact, I'm not even reconciled to myself, because I'm not reconciled to God. But when I am reconciled to God, then my true identity is available to be reconciled to my spouse.

Most people are familiar with the concept of reconciling a checkbook. In the old days, banks would send a statement of account to show transactions and balances according to their records. I would reconcile my statement by comparing my balance to theirs, and then account for any discrepancies. When there was a difference of opinion, the details had to be sorted out according to truth. The highest authority would establish the true value.

This is similar to being reconciled to God. He is the highest authority, so His opinion of our identity is the standard. We are not reconciled if our opinion differs from His. It is sin to hold a different opinion than God's, for it is the same as calling Him a liar. This is the reason that we become a new creation when we are reconciled to Him through Christ. We change our opinion of ourselves until it matches His, as the highest authority.

Being forgiven and reconciled to this new identity makes us free from guilt and condemnation, which otherwise would cause shame. When the cause of the shame is removed through reconciliation, for husband and wife, then it no longer affects how we see ourselves or each other. When she sees me, I am no longer the cause of shame in her. When I see myself, I am no longer the cause of shame in me.

We can't reconcile with sin because sin is anti-God. We can't be reconciled to God and at the same time be reconciled to something that is against God. It is impossible to reconcile to two different standards. I must be reconciled to God's standard, walk in that newness of life, and live as the new creation He has designed me to be. This is the act of repentance.

Mutual reconciliation requires that we accept one another, not calling our spouse back into an old identity nor holding her there. Just as we are being transformed by the renewing of our mind, we want to recognize, affirm and encourage transformation in our spouse. Therefore, we are being reconciled together with God.

Husbands and wives should esteem each other highly, living together according to the New Covenant. The reconciled relationship holds no debt against the other, except the ongoing debt of unconditional love.[31] A husband cannot demand this of his wife, nor a wife demand it from her husband, but each has responsibility in the sight of God in as much as they are able.[32]

We use this statement as a reminder of the reconciliation process: "God sees me as a new creation in Christ. Please agree with Him." It is a request that you agree with God's willingness and ability to forgive, transform, and cleanse from all un-righteousness.

This new identity allows innocence to be redeemed into purity. It was lost by sin and has been used by the accuser of the brethren to make a wedge come between husband and wife. It can be restored by giving and receiving forgiveness in our relationship. It restores the picture of what was supposed to be the relationship between us from the beginning. It approves us and operates as a promise that we can live in this kind of relationship, at peace with one another, and in that new identity. It is the preferable future that God had in mind even before you were conceived.

Spouses act as a mirror to one another. We reflect images back and forth. The bad news is that this can continually wound us, if the image being reflected only shows sin. The good news is that this can be very instructive to us. What we see in the physical realm is marred by sin. If that is all we can see in the other, then we cannot be reconciled. We cannot be merged as a couple.

God sees us as righteous, perfected by the love of Christ. When we see each other as God sees us, we have the opportunity to reflect that image back and forth to one another. What we see reflected then, is God's glory since we are created in His image. The more we mature in this, and the more we walk in this merged identity, the more accurately we reflect God's love to one another and back to God again. The glory of the Lord reflects and magnifies among God, husband and wife in the same way it has increased forever among the Triune Persons of God.

This is the picture of the ministry of reconciliation. It is the true love that covers a multitude of sins.[33] We demonstrate that love in our reconciled relationship with God. We demonstrate that love in our reconciled relationship with each other. Then our lives become a testimony of our loving and relational God and Heavenly Father to a watching world.

Homework Assignments

Take an accounting of offenses:

- Ask yourself: "What have I done that causes me guilt or shame?"
- Ask your spouse: "What have I done that caused you pain?"

Do an offense audit:

- Work together on the Father Assignment.
- Complete the Family of Origin Inventory. (Available at www.marriagerx.org).

Forgive each other from the heart

- Create a safe environment.
- Pray together that God will guide your conversation and guard your hearts.
- Introduce an event or offense that separates you.
- Discuss and identify the offense(s) that need to be forgiven.
- See to it that God has given forgiveness for each offense.
- Give and accept forgiveness as appropriate.
- Commemorate the transaction in a meaningful way.
- Repeat as necessary.

Chapter 5

Kinds of Relating

Developing Your Identity

The ways we relate to each other determine the kind of relationship we have. In a simple sense, relating means to have interaction between identities. It makes no sense on an individual level, but as soon as there are two or more identities, then a relationship exists. For example, God is relational because He is triune. Each person of the Trinity relates to the other persons. The identity of each person is defined in relationship to the others. Our marriages reflect this same truth.

We experience and demonstrate oneness as we treat each other with love. This is the mystery of merging two separate identities into one, and it only happens through the bond of love. If we are living separate lives, or parallel lives, we will always be fighting over control and power. Control can be expressed as domination, manipulation, or guidance. Power takes the form of fights, tension, or propulsion. In the one-flesh relationship power and control provide propulsion and guidance, but in a divided relationship it is conflict.

Two roles emerge in this environment of conflict: victim and villain. The victim is being controlled by another against his or her will. The villain is exercising control over the other. As long as control is vested in one person there cannot be a merger of identities. At first the villain uses control to dominate the victim, the weaker party. This may even be done by mutual consent, but the outcome is the denial of one identity in preference for the other. Control that is managed may not look like domination, but may resort to manipulation and coercion instead. The goal of love-based relating is to allow control to be the property of both husband and wife in the form of guidance.

At first glance we might assume that the villain is exercising all the power in the relationship, and the victim has none. This is not a true reflection of relationship, because each has power and exercises it. In an environment of conflict, the use of power is a fight. An imbalance of power makes one person a victim, but a balance of power creates a dynamic tension as each side pulls against the other. This tension is unhealthy as the relationship becomes strained even to the breaking point. In the one-flesh relationship we harness the power when each person contributes theirs for the common good. Then it becomes propulsion.

The godly marriage relationship allows each person to flourish, individually and as a couple. Like the Trinity, each person is distinct yet the union is inseparable. So it is with the one-flesh marriage in a healthy relationship. Each individual operates at his or her best, and as a couple they reflect that same success.

A marriage built in a worldly system assumes limited resources. When a husband and wife operate according to the world's economy, the best they can hope for is give and take. But each "take" is a deduction from the other's resources. At best, this leads to parallel lives and individualism. The Kingdom economy is based on give and receive because God has no limits to His resources. When one person gives to another it is not taken from his resources, but is received by the other.

When a husband and wife operate in a relationship that provides godly guidance instead of control, and supernatural propulsion instead of power struggles, they are unstoppable. This is God's idea of a marriage relationship, but first we need to see some of the ways that mankind has corrupted His plan.

Law-Based Relating

As we explore ways of relating, let's reconsider what we're trying to accomplish in our study. It isn't just learning to get along and have a long happy married life. Those are wonderful things, surely, but our goals need to be higher than that. Having a happy marriage aside, our goal as followers of Jesus is to model in the world the relationship that our Creator wishes to have with His creation. In other words, we are to live in such a way as to demonstrate the nature of God. The image of two people entering into a lifelong covenant depicts the eternal love relationship that God, the eternal bridegroom, has with His church, the bride.

Living that way requires us to evaluate the ways we try to get along in marriage, beginning with what we call, "law-based relating."

Marital Statutes

One of the most human of human habits is to develop habits.

Huh?

We create habits so that we can do things more efficiently, particularly those routine tasks like brushing our teeth or driving a car. The habits we develop make our daily lives easier.

In sports, habits are developed and refined so they become reflexes, as is the case in martial arts. An athlete trained in karate learns through careful repetition how to respond without thinking to the rapidly changing conditions of a competitive event. It would not do, as an opponent approaches, to have to consult one's notes to determine what block or other move might be appropriate—the match would be over before it began.

A doctor in a hospital emergency room needs to know what to do when a patient is brought in for treatment. What are the patient's injuries? Is the patient responding? Vital signs? What medical interventions should be used to save this life? Under such conditions, a doctor needs to know what must be done now, as it were, by instinct—habit.

The point is, we know the value of a predictable pattern and a habitual response.

So why not apply such principles to our marriage? Surely, by setting clearly defined rules to govern our married life we can avoid a lot of confusion and relate more efficiently. We can have a wonderful marriage if we just play by the rules.

Yes, but who makes the rules? The husband? Lots of men believe so...hope so. The wife? Surely she knows how things ought to be done. The problem here is that requiring our preferences from another feels less like a relationship and more like an arrangement. It may seem like rules would make things easier, but in reality they stand in the way of freedom in our relationship.

In an attempt to make things comfortable and predictable we create rules that govern all particulars, either explicitly or implicitly. Explicit rules are openly stated, laid out like a list of statutes to be obeyed—a line in the sand that is not to be crossed. Implicit rules are a moving target; we don't discover them until we have broken them somehow.

And that's true in any relationship, not just marriage.

The Mayhews have had numerous people, other than family members, live with them for over 35 years. Those relationships have ranged from blessing to challenging. One young fellow, who inquired about living with them, thoughtfully considered the room and other accommodations and, finding them adequate, explained that he was a student and would need to have the house quiet after 8:30 PM so he could study. He apparently had certain rules to govern relationships in his new living arrangement. Knowing that it would be easier to silence a hurricane than promise silence in their home (at almost any time, much less by 8:30) the Mayhews suggested their would-be boarder continue his search for more peaceful surroundings. Though the young man attempted to control his relationships in advance, his explicit rules were not the ticket to a new place to live.

Dan remembers another situation that occurred in the kitchen. While preparing his own breakfast he noted a renter's breakfast toast in the toaster. Thinking that it looked like it was getting close to burning, he gingerly lifted one of the slices in order to find out how close it might be to setting off the smoke alarm.

"Your toast might be getting a little overdone," he announced to his housemate. And that was the end of that.

He thought...

Later, as he sat seated at his desk in the basement, in came the renter, obviously upset. "I don't like people touching my food," she declared, and then went into a brief diatribe about her reasons.

Surprise! Who knew there was such a rule? Certainly not Dan, that is until it was broken. He was pleased to say that the infraction would not happen again. After all, how often in one lifetime is a person called upon to peek at someone else's toast? Fortunately, the toast incident was an exception and the relationship was not damaged in the long run. Things were only tense for a moment.

Both of these examples illustrate an attempt to govern relationship by rules. The first is preemptive, an attempt to govern behavior in advance. The second, is retroactive, an attempt to express displeasure by attaching it to a rule that was unknown to the violator until it had been broken. Both examples of law-based relating jeopardize healthy relationship by strangling it with fear (of breaking the rules) or with uncertainty.

Law is No Shortcut

When we introduce law into our marriage we think we are taking a shortcut to relationship by making things more predictable. Often, the exact opposite is true. Law makes the relationship edgy, fearful and eventually destructive. The problem with rules (laws) is that they start out as expectations directed at others, and expectations are nearly always disappointed and lead to disillusionment. Moreover, if we insist on our expectations they become demands, hardened like concrete. Demanding relationships ultimately reach a breaking point.

What is missing in law-based relationships is discernment, the careful consideration of the needs of another. If we are to perceive the needs of others we have to discard our own expectations and discern what is best for our partner and for the relationship. Evaluating behavior by rules and law is not discernment.

Let's look more closely at the anatomy of law-based relationships.

What happens if you get caught breaking the law, or when someone thinks you've broken the law? You get arrested. When that happens, you find yourself caught in a lot of legal machinery. It's no fun.

Let's say you are driving through an unfamiliar city and you get pulled over by a local police officer. You can tell he has some suspicions about what you're up to. Of course you protest that you were minding your own business; still the officer says you're under arrest for some kind of illegal activity—a theft, let's say.

He slaps the cuffs on you and hauls you off to the local jail where you wait for arraignment, which is your first appearance before the judge. The judge will evaluate you relative to the laws you are supposed to have broken.

The good news is that it's a case of mistaken identity. Of course you didn't do anything wrong. But if you had, the judge would have set your bail and you, quite probably would have to spend some time sitting in jail hoping you could figure out how to minimize the penalty you were facing if you were convicted.

Who are the characters in this little drama? You, of course—you're the defendant; the officer who observed you—he represents the law; and, finally, the judge. Those are the actors whenever laws are in place that can be broken.

These same characters are present in law-based relationships.

In a marriage that is law-based, there is a judge. And who might that be? The one who made the rule and believes that it should be observed if the marriage is to work properly. When a marriage rule is broken, then the judge steps forward and accuses the law-breaker. The penalty for the infraction is not measured in time served or fines levied, but in emotional currency like rejection and shame. In short, the law-keeper in the relationship plays more than one character. He/she is the accuser who feels wronged by the infraction (law enforcement) and the judge who is also the one who established the law in the first place. Often, a partner that steps into this role is deemed judgmental and always fixing blame, or even shifting blame from themselves to another.

The one who broke the rule (and remember the rule may not have been very apparent) becomes the "defendant," the one accused. Note the root word "defend" or "defense." Even the word suggests the likely outcome in this law-based interaction: defensiveness.

Another result of playing the defendant role is self-centeredness. Why?

A number of years ago, the Mayhews hosted in their home a fellow who illustrates this point. He was a capable young man with multiple talents. Among them, by his own analysis, was that he was a "problem solver"—an admirable skill. There was a dilemma, though. To recognize a problem required that he be convinced of how things ought to be done, otherwise how would he know that there was a problem to solve? Consequently, he was often unhappy with the way things were done around the house. He had a list—an implicit list of laws—which could be violated at any time. While he wasn't in a position to mete out consequences, he would point out the deficiencies in the household, or suggest his doubts in more subtle ways, that eventually led members of the household to wonder where they would fall short next. Eventually, they found themselves becoming self-centered, constantly evaluating themselves against the hidden standards of the judge in the home. Are we OK? What would he say about this? Is this what he meant when he said...?

From this experience, Dan is often heard to warn, "Beware of the man with a ruler in his pocket!" Such people are always ready to measure others by their standard, resulting in defensiveness and self-centeredness in the ones he judges. This is true in many kinds of communities, but is most destructive in a marriage.

Results of Law-based Relationships

Would it be accurate to say that having judges and defendants in your marriage is not a recipe for a successful union? Yes. In relationships based on rules, love and acceptance are based on performance, with the result that when performance is disappointing, love and acceptance are withheld. And it doesn't stop there.

Living in a law-based environment changes our behavior in multiple ways. Adaptable creatures that we are, we tend to adjust our practices to protect our emotions and to secure, if possible, a positive opinion from others. The more constraining our social environment, the more disguised we become. Rather than reveal our true feelings and risk being accused or condemned, we tend to play the chameleon and become something more suitable to our partner, avoiding those unpleasant visits to the courtroom. We pretend we are someone we are not in order to keep the peace. That is not freedom, which is the condition God created humans to live in; it is bondage. Living in the condition of being controlled and limited by others, has two outcomes: resignation leading to passive withdrawal, or resentment leading to rebellion.

Sadly, we have seen law-based marriage relationships in which the partners have all but given up being transparent and real. In situations where both husband and wife try to rule one another by law, the relationship often becomes distant and settles into "parallel lives"—together but not touching at a heart level. The two withdraw into an uneasy peace and bitter resignation that nothing will change. In more lop-sided marriages where one spouse consistently dominates the other, the outcome is more dramatic.

In the case of a relationship where one partner is consistently dominated by the other and becomes resigned to the situation—hopelessly outmatched—the result is a sacrifice of personality. There was a couple who had been married for nearly ten years. Their relationship was characterized by emotional manipulation by the wife. If her husband failed to meet her expectations in some way, she would either lash out verbally or engage in some kind of punitive behavior like pouting or withholding communication.

For his part, he had given up. To keep the peace, he declined to object to her behavior while he did everything he could to pacify her moods. The result was a lifeless marriage and a husband whose personality was colorless and without hope. Around the house he was nervous and unmotivated. In social situations he was silent, nearly invisible. His personality had become totally eclipsed by his domineering and judgmental spouse.

Some law-based relationships have a quite different result: retaliation and rebellion.

According to scripture, law has a way of provoking that kind of reaction. In Paul's letter to the church in Rome, he makes this observation:

> For the law brings wrath, because where there is
> no law there is no transgression either. [1]

In context, Paul is talking about the Old Testament law that Jesus came to complete, but he identifies a principle that applies to our discussion about relating. It is this: when there is law in place, then there is the potential for it to be broken. Law disobeyed results in wrath, a negative reaction. Similarly, Paul wrote in his letter to the Romans:

> But sin, seizing the opportunity through the
> commandment, produced in me all kinds of wrong
> desires. For apart from the law, sin is dead. [2]

The outcome of imposing law in some marriages is far from passive and withdrawn. Sometimes it is exactly the opposite. Sometimes, the law-based condition can persist just so long before the relationship becomes reactive rather than responsive.

There is a pronounced difference between a reaction and a response. Reacting is like a ball hurled against the floor, it bounces back with almost equal force. In a relationship, we react when we feel threatened or defensive. A response, on the other hand, is a measured answer to the circumstances based on our awareness that we are bound by a covenant, the commitment to act for the benefit of our partner.

In a reactionary relationship, either or both of the parties is on the defensive and ready to make an aggressive stand against accusation and judgment. That defensive, "high alert" status makes quarreling and disunity inevitable, even over relatively minor issues.

Dan remembers a counseling appointment with a woman who reported that she had nearly committed suicide recently. He asked her what circumstances had driven her to that serious moment. She described what happened.

Her husband announced that he was going to the store to pick up a few things. She asked if he would pick up a pack of cigarettes, a half pint of half 'n half and a dozen eggs. A half hour later, he called from the store to ask about the list. He remembered the cigarettes and the eggs, but what was that third thing?

The woman's reaction was disproportionate to the offense. Why don't you pay attention when I tell you things? How come you're only careless about what I want? You never think about what I need, only about yourself! The conversation ended with a shouting match, a violent hanging up of the phone and the woman staring at her reflection in the bathroom mirror, a bottle of prescription pills in her hand.

What? Over a half pint of half 'n half? Of course not. The reaction erupted out of a long history of expectations, demands and unspoken rules that had eventually awakened sin of every kind in the marriage.

A responsive relationship, one that draws from mutual respect and freedom, is the product of covenant, which is the reflection of the faith relationship that exists between God and His church. Such a relationship is not the result of a rigid set of rules that keeps the parties in line; it is the reflection of love, acceptance and forgiveness that is present in God. It is a dynamic and mutually beneficial relationship that is lived out of freedom and not slavery; in truth, not pretense. As Jesus said, "you shall know that truth and the truth will set you free." [3]

Paul expanded the idea further.

> For you did not receive the spirit of slavery leading again to fear, but you received the Spirit of adoption, by whom we cry, "Abba, Father." [4]

Though he references the parent-child relationship, Paul has captured the nature of the covenant relationship into which God has invited His creation, one of freedom and not slavery. Elsewhere he simply states that "where the Spirit of the Lord is, there is liberty." [5]

God has invited us into a covenant relationship with Him and then has commissioned us to demonstrate that relationship to the world through marriage. If we are going to be effective communicators of this important dimension of God's love, there is not room for law, accusation and judgment in our relationship. Instead, we are to learn from Christ's example of humble servanthood and live together in the condition that He died to secure for us. Paul described it this way:

> For freedom Christ has set us free. Stand firm, then, and do not be subject again to the yoke of slavery. [6]

Shame-Based Relating

Shame is used in law-based relating as a tool to exercise power or control. Law based relating has to do with judgment compared to a standard, or law. When we are in the role of villain in a law-based relationship we have no authority of our own, and so we must appeal to a higher authority. We appeal to the law, or more accurately to our interpretation of the law, and in that way control the standard. We exercise control and power over others when we hold them to our standard, or our will, through judgment and condemnation.

The message is: "You are a law breaker." It doesn't matter if the message is spoken or implied, it is used to destroy the other person's identity. Shaming, that is proclaiming shame on another, defines them in contrast to the law. We recoil from anything that causes shame because it reminds us of our sin nature.

Shame has power over us when we are measured against a standard and found wanting. The controller defines the standard and measures the performance. He is interested in the gap between the standard and performance so he can use the shortfall as a basis for shame.

"I thought you were better than that." This observation is a very subtle form of coercion. It implies that the victim must improve and modify their behavior or live under the shame of not measuring up. In a less subtle way it is saying: "You are not meeting my expectations for you. Shame on you for failing to perform properly."

The villain is not interested in compliance. No matter how hard the victim tries to measure up, they cannot. The villain will raise the standard because it is not meant to be met, it is only useful to create the failure gap. The victim is seeking approval or acceptance but receives shame instead.

Honor is one of the common standards used in shame-based relating. It begins with an unspoken assumption that honor is the opposite of shame. Frequently it relates to the honor of the villain or the family. Quite common are accusations that the failure in performance will destroy, or has destroyed, the honor of the family. More subtly are inferred judgments such as: "People are looking," or "You are not going to amount to anything." The force in shaming-based on honor is the implication that the victim is to blame for the lack of honor.

Phantom standards are those that cannot be pinned down and creep higher and higher to stay ahead of performance. This is a common ploy of the controller, especially when the victim is desperate to please them or get approval. As soon as the person meets the standard the villain raises it. The victim tries even harder to meet that, and the cycle continues. There is no end because the gap must be there for the control to work.

There are other unattainable standards used in shame-based relating, like the comment: "Why can't you be like your brother?" The implied standard is that the victim be as acceptable as his brother. Since the victim cannot be his brother it is impossible to achieve this standard. At the same time, the shamer defines the level of acceptability and has already indicated that the victim does not measure up. No matter what he does, he will never be like his brother.

One other example of an unattainable standard comes in the form of a question: "Are you doing everything you can?" This is a rhetorical question that assumes a negative answer. The accusation is that the victim is not doing everything he can and therefore deserves shame. It is impossible to define "everything you can" because the standard can be raised unendingly, in theory.

Shame-based relating can happen in a Christian context just as often as in a worldly one. As villain, we hold up the commandments and will of God as the standard. Then we judge the victim as having failed that standard and therefore worthy of shame. We act as if our judgment is perfect and that God is on our side. This is the root of spiritual abuse, in defiance of the command to not judge others.

The villain uses the threat of shame to control the victim. This can be overt shame, such as requiring the victim to wear a demeaning sign or label. It can also be shame expressed verbally: "Shame on you!" However, shame based relating can also sneak in undetected.

The threat of disapproval might not be verbalized. It can be communicated with a look, a breath, or a gesture. A raised eyebrow or wrinkled nose warns the victim that he is unacceptable. Married couples have history and experience that can make the most subtle signal witheringly effective. Withholding a compliment or smile can be more devastating than lodging a complaint.

Families and groups can use the threat of disloyalty to power shame-based relating. This threat is effective when loyalty, or the appearance of loyalty, is valued by the group. "Don't make the family look bad." "Protect our reputation." These are examples of shaming messages used to control behavior.

"You'll never be mother of the year." This shaming statement uses the threat of disqualification. The loss of a potential position, title or role is projected as current failure. Shame is placed on the victim to control or manipulate based on the assumed goal of achieving that title or role.

There are some common symptoms that indicate shame-based relating. One significant clue is a relationship built on performance or works. The members in the relationship attempt to earn approval by the things they do and the ways they do them. The religious example of this is a person trying to overcome the wages of sin by the work they do, hoping that God will find them acceptable. Marriages can be built on a similar model, though no amount of works or effort will ever suffice since the way the couple relates is about control rather than love.

For example, a husband wants to care for his wife and does so by working hard at his job to get promoted or to qualify for a raise. His motive is to provide for his family, and the compelling factor is to be acceptable. His wife wishes he would help out with raising the family and resents his long hours at work. She shames him for what is left undone and he tries to make it up through the efforts he thinks are most important. Miscommunication on these points can derail a marriage.

Perfectionists and procrastinators can also be trapped in shame-based relating. These characteristics are regularly found in people that grew up in a shaming household. The two behaviors are cousins of the same coping strategy. Perfectionists attempt to get everything exactly right so no failure can be assigned to them. Procrastinators have learned to postpone a project so they are not overwhelmed by the pressure of being perfect. They console themselves by saying they did as well as they could in the time allowed.

People that are trapped in shame-based relationships may have failure due to their fear of failure. Their experience has been that nothing is good enough. No matter how hard they try, they will never measure up. Rather than try to overcome the shame, they give up in hopelessness. This kind of relating will not bring out the best in your spouse.

One other very common symptom of shame-based relating is a critical spirit. Carriers of this spirit are quick to measure others against some standard and judge them as inadequate. They are not intending to shame anyone else, but it is an unavoidable frame of reference. They may try to soften the blow by admitting they are their own worst critic. That does not help them, or the person they are judging.

Shame-based relating often originates from generational influence. When a person grows up in a household that has used shame as a tool for compliance or control, then that pattern is brought into their marriage. When children are born to this couple, it is likely that they will learn this behavior and bring it to the next generation in similar fashion.

It can also arise when a person feels shame for failing to perform to a standard they have set. Usually this failure is self-interpreted and the feeling self-assigned. They attempt to control their own behavior in hopes of avoiding further shame. This becomes the basis for relationship when they share the shame with others.

The antidote is to live according to your identity in Christ. This is the new standard. Then you are not trying to live up to the expectations of another, or your own interpretation of the law, but how God sees you. When you live that way you measure up. You are righteous.[7]

Secondly, accept your spouse according to his or her identity in Christ. Do not accept your spouse as you hope she will become, but as the person God created her to be. Christ has given her a reputation to live up to, give her encouragement to do so.

Next, give and receive unrestricted forgiveness for failures. There is no shame in forgiveness. When failure happens, offer forgiveness and then there is no foothold for shame. Practice this with your spouse, your children, your extended family, even your in-laws.

Finally, develop a generous spirit. This is the opposite of a critical spirit and takes away the power of shaming. Create a generous spirit through thanksgiving. Give thanks for what it is, not what it could be. When you have a grateful attitude and a generous spirit you have created a hostile environment for shame.

Both law-based and shame-based relating are methods to control another in a relationship by squashing their identity instead of allowing it to grow in freedom.

Need-Based Relating

Several years ago, an American film, a love story, popularized a phrase that was applied to the relationship in the movie. As the man and woman grew closer in their relationship, one finally said to the other, "you *complete* me." The suggestion in the phrase is that until the two met, at least one of the pair was incomplete, somehow only a fragment of a whole being. The assumption was that both regarded the other as that elusive missing piece that prevented them from realizing their full personhood.

The phrase describes a relationship that may be headed for trouble. Why? After all "you complete me" sounds so...so....romantic. How could there be a problem with it?

First, the phrase reveals something about each partner's understanding of themselves, namely that they need something that another person must give if they are to be whole. It starts with an expectation.

Second, it assumes that both partners feel the same way, when he or she may not. While one partner is satisfied that his or her relational needs are met, the other is conveying a relentless sense of needing or wanting something. The more intense that need, the more demanding the needy partner may seem, or actually be.

The issue in play here is lust.

Lust? Why apply this ugly sounding word to relationships based on need? To explore the reasons, let's take a look at a well-known passage from the Bible, specifically the book of James. For purposes of this discussion, let's imagine that James is making reference to married people. It does a good job of describing need-based relating.

> What is the source of quarrels and conflicts among you? Is not the source your pleasures that wage war in your members? You lust and do not have ...

you are envious and cannot obtain, so you fight and quarrel. You do not have because you do not ask. You ask and do not receive, because you ask with wrong motives, so that you may spend it on your pleasures. You adulteresses, do you not know that friendship with the world is hostility toward God? Therefore whoever wishes to be a friend of the world makes himself an enemy of God. Or do you think that the Scripture speaks to no purpose: "He jealously desires the Spirit which He has made to dwell in us"? But He gives a greater grace. Therefore it says, "GOD IS OPPOSED TO THE PROUD, BUT GIVES GRACE TO THE HUMBLE." Submit therefore to God. Resist the devil and he will flee from you. Draw near to God and He will draw near to you. Cleanse your hands, you sinners; and purify your hearts, you double-minded.[8]

Taken in the context of marriage, in the verses above there appear to be three persons in the relationship. Two people and God; God is very much a part of this discussion of need-based relationships. So why do relationships struggle with neediness when we're supposed to be walking with God?

The book of James is pretty explicit about the source of conflict: lust. Whenever the goal of a person in a relationship is to gain from the other person what only God can supply, stresses begin to appear in the relationship. When a needy heart, on a quest to be complete, reaches out for a person or thing rather than coming to wait on God for those needs, it frequently places a burden on the spouse who, inevitably, will be unable to satisfy all needs all the time. Eventually, humans fail to live up to expectations and that failure becomes a source of strife and conflict.

Lust and Desire

In an earlier chapter we wrote about the relationship between two words: desire and lust. Interestingly, depending on the context, both words are translated from the same Greek word: *epithumeo*. In many translations, if the word is used in the context of seeking after God and His will, the word is translated, desire. When it is used to describe coveting or clamoring after a thing for personal benefit, it is translated, lust. Moreover, if we express our desire toward God, our relationships with other people will be appropriate, but if our desire is not fixed on the Lord, and we don't know how to have our needs addressed in the context of a relationship with Him, then we will be looking outwardly toward the world to get those needs met. That is when the word becomes, 'lust.' As long as we are looking outside of the three relationships within marriage, and particularly when we marginalize the critical relationship with God, then there will be a constant sense of neediness that, when turned on our spouse, can evolve into a demand that they meet our needs. Or, just as bad, our expectations can sink lower and lower until we come to live with a sense of hopelessness. Either way, it becomes lust when we begin to look to other people and evaluate how well they may meet our requirements.

Those consequences are the result of neglecting what Jesus taught: "Seek first the kingdom of God and all these things will be added unto you." Looking for kingdom benefits in the world or in other people is bound to be fruitless. Moreover, the result of seeking Him first will be an appropriate relationship with others.

Nobody starts out in a marriage intending to be needy. We don't enter into a relationship consciously expecting to have the other person meet our needs. That doesn't stop us from doing that very thing unconsciously. How does this happen? It is important to answer this question for ourselves because, the minute we begin to find ways to meet our need that do not come from that central relationship with our Creator, then we begin to feed lust, which then creates an appetite.

The problem with appetites is that when they are fed, they tend to increase. They just don't go away. Perhaps you have had the experience of finding a new piece of furniture or décor for your home. Have you noticed that getting something new has a way of making everything else look old by comparison? You may intend to be satisfied with whatever you brought into the room, but there is the temptation to add another improvement to go with each new addition. Once that second thing is added...well, you get the picture. Feeding an appetite doesn't satisfy it.

Dark Strategy

This is where the strategy of the evil forces comes into the picture. When we are enticed toward being need oriented—motivated by lust—it is fairly easy for us to be taken off course and guided by what our body or emotions want. The proper course originates from a "kingdom" orientation that emanates from our relationship with the Lord. Unless appetites are satisfied by a rich inner life, they will become the source of conflict in a relationship, whether marriage or even in a church.

The word that is commonly used to describe this lust and need-based relating is "co-dependency." Such relationships are characterized by, "I need you. I want you. I have to have you in my life to meet my needs." When our daughters (the Mayhews) prepared to go off to college, we made it a point to offer a bit of parental advice. We told them that if a young man came along who told them that he needed them, wanted them, could not live without them, they should run in the opposite direction as fast as they could. Such declarations of love are based on the needs of the young man, who has seen something that he wants for himself; to consume on his own needs. The needs of the young lady are not topmost in his mind.

So, how do you recognize that this dynamic has begun to operate in your marriage? In a marital relationship, the problems don't originate in something that one or the other spouse lacks, but from the way each party intends to have those needs met. If a husband has a sense of need in his life that he feels can only be met by his wife, he has missed the mark. The meeting of his needs must start with his inner relationship with God, not with his outer relationship with his wife. If he fails to realize this, his needs may become expectations aimed at his wife. They will easily become demands. He may even try to manipulate their relationship. Whatever strategy that he decides to use to get his needs met, they will weaken the relationship with his spouse. Furthermore, when unmet needs become the focus of the relationship, and God is not central to the meeting of those needs, then lust becomes the operator. One of the dangers of lust is that it often misdirects us toward a substitute for the real desire.

We all have a need for love that is built in to us from the very beginning. It is a reflection of the love that exists among the persons of the Trinity. If our need for love becomes misdirected, it can easily look to sex as a substitute, whether an extramarital affair or pornography. Healthy relationship is love-based, but if it becomes need-based, it can easily give place to lust. This misdirects our God-given need for love to the consumption of another person via sex, which easily impersonates love. Sex is designed to be the seal of love, yet in our culture it is reshaped by lust into a means of personal pleasure and little more.

Another outcome of need-based relating is a relationship that becomes exclusive and consuming. The parties become so intent on taking what they need from one another—classic codependency—that there is no time left for other friendships. No time for family. Little time for social engagement of any kind if it might take away from the time spent together. In such relationships, if one or the other spouse (or unmarried friends) should dare to extend outside of the exclusive boundary, anger and manipulation often erupt between them. Then, true to the scriptural principle, "the sun goes down on your anger"[9] in the relationship, creating a foothold for the enemy, and making room for jealousy and simmering resentment. Such scenarios, not infrequently, end up in divorce or emotional estrangement.

In the past, Jody has done a significant amount of counseling, particularly among women who struggled with sexual brokenness in their lives. Frequently, that brokenness manifested itself in unhealthy relationships that were need-based. The more she encountered these unhealthy patterns, she began to wonder if there was a way to dig into a person's history and discover the true need that had gone unmet and led to seeking fulfillment in unhealthy ways. And, how did these patterns play out when people approached marriage, arriving at that important decision with baggage filled with neediness.

As she pondered that question she realized that the answer would not be found in analyzing the broken areas in a person's life—their current condition. She determined that the better approach was to start with the basic needs that God intended to be met in each of us and then discern what patterns had been adopted in an attempt to overcome any deficiencies.

A Cup Half Full

Let's illustrate it this way. Imagine an empty cup to represent a child's life. God's intention is for that cup to be filled with certain essential components added by a mother and father, day upon day, until the child reaches a point of healthy maturity. We don't know, necessarily, when that age is. In the animal kingdom the longest period of time a parent nurtures its young is about two years—relatively brief compared to humans. For humans, it's not uncommon for the process to continue for 20 years, sometimes more. During that time, it is God's intention for the heart of a child to be filled with essential tools for successful living. Parents are to be pouring into their child's heart socially, mentally, emotionally, spiritually and a dozen other ways—day upon day the pouring continues.

If that process proceeds as it was designed, the child's "life-cup" is filling up until the child reaches healthy independence. But, often, that isn't the pattern. Often, there are significant deficiencies—gaps—in preparation. Sadly, most of us reach the moment of independence with a cup that is, at least partially empty.

When I (Jody) was growing up, I was the only child in a school of about 300 students who came from what, in those days, was called "a broken home." By the time our second daughter was in first grade, she was one of only four in her class that was living with both birth parents, in other words, an intact home. Clearly, the societal shift is away from the pattern of two parents pouring into the life of the offspring that they brought into the world. Moreover, as most children today grow to independence and then seek a life partner, it will be increasingly rare for both partners to come from such parents.

So, what happens when the pattern is interrupted; when either mom or dad is taken out of the picture?

It should be said here, that there are multiple reasons that a parent is not available to pour into a child. Divorce is only one. Abandonment also occurs when there is a death in the family or when drugs and alcohol invade the home. A parent may be a workaholic; addicted to technology or the internet; or merely consumed by personal interests. A distracted parent is unavailable. Add to the list, abuse, (physical, sexual or verbal) or family violence—any of these may cause a child to withdraw from relationship. In other words, even if a parent is not gone physically from the home, there are reasons why a child may not be receiving what is necessary to fill their cup.

When that happens, when one parent becomes unavailable, there is a line drawn and valuable resources are withheld from the child. At that point, the child may begin to compensate by discovering ways of filling what is lacking to make up for his own internal neediness.

Returning to our cup illustration, let water represent the positive contribution of the parents. It rises to a certain level and then stops when one parent becomes disconnected from the family. The child, then, begins to make his or her own contributions to compensate. Let ping-pong balls represent those coping skills. Most of us have at least a few ping-pong balls in our lives. They fill up the cup.

The problem with ping-pong balls, though, is they are empty. What they make up in volume, they lack in content. Something is missing. Consequently, if the child is quite young when a parent leaves the family, symptoms may look like a regression—a return to wetting the bed, for example. An adolescent, on the other hand, will show a different set of markers, such as intensified rebellion or risk-taking behaviors.

That isn't to say that all self-actualized survival skills are bad. Some seem to be quite good—are quite good. The class clown is everybody's favorite—fun to be with. The top performer in school is the one everyone wants on the team, or cheers for on the field. In the workplace, there are employees that stand out, rising through the ranks to pull down the top salary while helping the company thrive. Positive survival skills often pop up in Christian environments where spiritual activities, charitable work and general busyness around the church are considered valuable, to be encouraged and emulated.

But outward appearance, as the saying goes, can be deceiving. The class clown may well be masking inner feelings of abandonment and rejection by inviting the laughter and appreciation of classmates. More than one successful comedian has confessed to having a dismal childhood. The star athlete or the upwardly mobile employee may be riding a wave of perfectionism, seeking the respect and admiration of others to compensate for the lack of those same things in their family. In the church, the spiritual dynamo may be secretly wondering if any of it is enough; whether God is judging all the effort and finding it lacking; imagining others in the community criticizing in the shadows.

The problem with creating our own survival skills is often we are privately aware that they are empty—ping-pong balls. We have a hidden sense of our own neediness. We know it's there even if others do not. All of the positive activities are filling the cup, but the cup is not really full. All of the diversions and vices give momentary relief but do nothing to fill the emptiness.

Surely, God does not intend that lives be lived half full. There must be another way of making up for the lack that so many of us live with. Otherwise all of our relationships, in the end, will be need-based as we helplessly try to gain from others what is missing.

A Cup Running Over

Our Father intends to re-parent us, to fill up what has been left out, but not from the outside. He comes from within us saying, "from out of your innermost being will come rivers of living water." [10] When He comes to father us, to bring us to well-being and maturity, *He does it from within.* Now, imagine the result if, day upon day, our cup begins to be filled up with water. What happens to the ping-pong balls—those coping skills? As the water rises, one by one, the ping-pong balls— our compensations—are displaced and replaced. But that all depends on our willingness to yield to Him and let Him meet the needs that only He can meet instead of reaching out horizontally, to behaviors or to other people to have our needs met that way.

In Paul's second letter to the church in Corinth, the apostle is responding to his experience with the community there.

> For I fear that perhaps when I come I may find you not as I wish, and that you may find me not as you wish--that perhaps there may be quarreling, jealousy, anger, hostility, slander, gossip, conceit, and disorder. I fear that when I come again my God may humble me before you, and I may have to mourn over many of those who sinned earlier and have not repented of the impurity, sexual immorality, and sensuality that they practiced. [11]

The good news, here, is that even the church of the first century seems to have been challenged by the same weaknesses that we experience. At least we are not alone. The bad news is that we are still being challenged by them!

How can that be? Why are we consistently, both then and now, inclined to reach out to others to meet our needs in ways that only God is in a position to do? Is there no hope for getting beyond ourselves?

Part of the problem grows from a fundamental misunderstanding of this scripture:

> Now concerning the matters about which you wrote: "It is good for a man not to have sexual relations with a woman." But because of the temptation to sexual immorality, each man should have his own wife and each woman her own husband. The husband should give to his wife her conjugal rights, and likewise the wife to her husband. For the wife does not have authority over her own body, but the husband does. Likewise the husband does not have authority over his own body, but the wife does. Do not deprive one another, except perhaps by agreement for a limited time, that you may devote yourselves to prayer; but then come together again, so that Satan may not tempt you because of your lack of self-control. Now as a concession, not a command, I say this. I wish that all were as I myself am. But each has his own gift from God, one of one kind and one of another. To the unmarried and the widows I say that it is good for them to remain single as I am. But if they cannot exercise self-control, they should marry. For it is better to marry than to be aflame with passion. [12]

Often this passage is taught as a biblical instruction on how to deal with lust; a way of dealing with being needy in the area of sexual gratification. Marriage is the answer to the need-based experience of lust.

What? Is that really what Paul is saying?

To get a clearer picture of what is being taught, note Paul's reference to himself and to his decisions in the matter.

Apparently, Paul was unmarried and had chosen to remain so. He had decided that this portion of his life should be sacrificed for the sake of the gospel so he could more fully pursue his calling as an apostle. In fact, this is the key to what this passage is about. Sexuality is to be laid on the altar before the Lord; it is not to be understood as a remedy for the neediness of lust. These verses are an instruction on how to pledge one's whole self for the gospel. A single person sacrifices physical needs as Paul did, unto the Lord. But, Paul makes it clear that, even if abstinence seems too great a burden, sacrifice must still take place in the context of the covenant of marriage. "Your body doesn't belong to you any more," says Paul. "It belongs to your spouse." This is how, as a married person, a Christian devotes his sexuality to the Lord: by giving up authority over his or her body. This is how all followers of the Lord can learn the worship of sacrifice.

If we don't understand Paul's instruction in this way, then it becomes nothing more than a "legal loophole" for need-based relating; an invitation for an appetite, demanding to be fed, to come into marriage. Lust would be given full reign to seek its own satisfaction and eclipse the fulfillment of the preeminent human need, the need to worship. That is the core truth that Paul is teaching, that our sexual need is to be an offering to the Lord and to one another. Sexuality is something not taken for ourselves, but given; it is a component of our being that we are invited to sacrifice in the environment of selflessness and covenant.

Fear-Based Relating

If any of these modes of relating are active in our relationship then there will be fear. The key to authentic relating in a relationship is freedom, and when there is an absence of freedom in a relationship there is going to be *fear-based relating*.

There are different types of fear, and not all fear is harmful. In fact, it is a very important tool for our protection. What is harmful is when fear is a scheme of the devil. We read in the book of Hebrews that Christ came to destroy the power of the devil and free those who have been held in slavery by their fear of death.[13] If we are afraid of death then we are held in slavery by that fear. The fear of death is the root of many fears and it motivates us toward self-protection.

The fear of death can also be considered a fear of loss. The loss of life triggers in some the fear of loss of identity, loss of personhood, loss of choice, and loss of future. In the physical realm these are all true. This demonstrates the relationship between death and loss. We can apply this way of thinking to other fears and thereby gain a better understanding of its power.

The fear of pain is related to the fear of death because it is a poignant reminder of the dying process. Fear of abandonment is a fear of loss, or death, of relationships. Fear of rejection comes from the loss of acceptance. Fear of failure stems from a potential loss of reputation. We can apply this thought process to any fear.

There is a fear to be encouraged: the fear of the Lord.[14] This kind of fear leads to reverence and is the beginning of wisdom. We were designed to put our fear in the greatest thing. In fact, whatever is perceived as the greatest threat (fear) will be held at the top of our mind, according to those that study how humans think. It will be held in that position until it is resolved. That means we are at risk of putting our fear in the wrong place. This is a warning: if we fear anything besides the Lord we are assigning it a greater role in our life than God, and that is idolatry.

The fear of the unknown can be put in a class by itself. It is most closely related to the fear of loss of control or a perceived death of will through lack of reason. Of course this assumes that with proper warning, sufficient time and information we are going to make the best choices, and that lacking these resources we are likely to err. This is typical of western thought, and makes us most susceptible to this fear.

There are two roles in fear-based relating: victim and villain. The victim gives away control out of fear. We talked about commitment levels in the first chapter, and a victim is one that is 100% committed to the other person. As a victim I live my life so the other person won't leave me, hate me, or hurt me. It is all focused on how I can please you or appease you so I will avoid pain.

The villain refuses to acknowledge another's free will and attempts to control their identity. This is a case of being 100% committed to me. As villain we are making sure our needs get met at the other's expense, using fear to control you, to live your life for you, so you won't leave me, hate me, or hurt me. It is all focused on how I can get you to please or appease me so I will avoid pain.

The villain uses intimidation to exercise control. Threats of physical pain are pretty obvious and play right into the victim's fear of death or the dying process. Physical abuse can play a role in this, but not necessarily. Often a villain uses posturing, threatening gestures, or overwhelming presence to communicate the possibility of pain. We experienced this in a troubled relationship where the husband was a very big man and the wife a rather slight woman. Though he had never struck her or physically forced her, he allowed her to believe that it could happen at any moment. She responded in the same kind of fear as if he had a history of physically abusing her.

Another common villain strategy plays into the victim's fear of the unknown. Key phrases include: "You don't want to go there!" or "You will, or else ..." These veiled threats take advantage of the way the victim's imagination escalates the risk in an attempt to avoid pain.

The victim uses abdication to avoid control. They believe that exercising control makes them responsible for their pain or the pain of others. The fear of pain drives them to dodge detection, fly under the radar, fit in or disappear. In relationships, they attempt to mitigate conflict by managing everything according to the assumed standards or demands of the villain. They try to appease by denying themselves.

A common issue of fear is to interpret normal things as a threat. Our society operates in fear and anxiety so much of the time that we think it is normal. We don't think fear is optional, but that it is to be expected. It takes form as fear for health, fear in finances, fear about relationships, fear regarding the future, and so on. Since this is a prevalent worldview, it is hard to escape. The victim is set up for being manipulated because of this worldview. For instance, it is normal to put effort into work or role, but the victim turns this into motivation by fear of failure. It is normal to desire health and pursue joy, but the victim turns this into motivation by fear of sickness. It is prudent to save for emergencies or future plans, but the victim turns this into motivation by fear of poverty.

This worldview of pending failure leads the victim into fear of responsibility. We have observed that this usually begins at an early age, influenced by the family of origin. The victim has no practical experience in making decisions, no confidence in his ability, and sometimes he is not able to access his own ideas, preferences or desires. He does not have an opinion, nor does he know how to form one.

Watch for these common symptoms of fear-based relating in your marriage or family. First of all, if everything is perceived through a grid of fear and anxiety, then all choices and decisions will reflect that worldview. Decisions will be motivated by avoiding risk, and choices will be justified by how effective they are deemed to be at protecting those involved. Characterizing every situation by the perceived severity of its risk is a sure sign of fear-based thinking.

Another common symptom is when one or more people in the relationship are reluctant to make a decision. Each attempts to avoid the responsibility of risk, as if the risk itself were unavoidable. We have seen some very clever maneuvering between husband and wife so that the responsibility of a decision falls on someone else. It can be cloaked in timidity, politeness, humility, or generosity, but the real motive is fear.

Fear is a lousy guard. It is given to us for protection, but operating in fear does not prevent us from being hurt or experiencing pain. The idea that we can avoid it by worry or fear is a lie. Instead, fear puts us at odds with each other. When we are fearful, we can project that fear on others as well. This is one way that fear infects our spouse, children, friends, and co-workers. The opposite is also true, that we can ascribe fear to another because of our worldview. Our fear-based thinking attributes a fear motive to others, even if they do not deserve it.

Anger is often a guardian emotion for the person that is hiding fear. It may feel safe for them to control their situation with an outburst of anger rather than appear weak in fear. The opposite reaction is withdrawal for the person that is hiding fear. Anger and withdrawal are each responses to fear, but on opposite sides of a continuum. The response a person chooses has to do with their basic personality, measured as flight or fight response, as well as the situation. If your marriage struggles with anger issues or timidity and isolation, then investigate your areas of fear.

We were ministering to a fear-based couple some time ago. The wife feared her husband, especially because of his anger management issues. She was confused when we asked what he was afraid of. She assured us that he was afraid of nothing. Later we were able to minister to her husband, and asked him what he was afraid of. He was afraid she would leave him. He used anger to control her and cover up his greater fear, and in so doing was driving her away. God healed them of their fears, and they were amazed at how powerfully it had been working against them.

Fear-based relating is about control. The villain uses fear to override the victim's free will. The victim avoids fear and is thereby manipulated. It would appear that the roles are relatively fixed, but that is not the case. Sometimes we see people compete for the victim role in a relationship. Each perceives the other as having all the power or control or authority, and in response they abdicate responsibility. The roles of villain and victim flip flop as each tries to mitigate risk, and each ascribes all the power and control to the other.

What then is the antidote to fear-based relating?

The first step is to face the fear, identify it, and bring it out into the open. This seems counter-intuitive when we are trying to avoid it, but we must seek the truth because the truth sets us free. Hiding from fear does not make it less powerful, quite to the contrary. However, facing the fear reverses the tendency to escalate the fear in our imagination. When the fear is required to stand on its own merit, then we can trust God to help us accept the risk. Fear loses its power in this exchange.

Fear of the unknown loses its power when we are willing to be naked and unashamed. As you recall from the third chapter, this removes all hiding strategies that would be the platform from which fear is born. In this state we can be vulnerable to the fear and each other. This too is counter-intuitive, but very effective. Openness removes the implicit power of fear.

We have discovered that there is a root cause of being a victim or villain in a relationship, and this must be resolved from the inside out. Too often married couples work on the issues and symptoms instead of dealing with the cause of the problem. Fear keeps us from looking inside, but that is where God wants to heal us.

We cannot have an authentic naked and unashamed relationship if one is a victim and another a villain. Authenticity in relationship must come through a place of freedom. As we recognize our freedom in Christ we can relate authentically with one another as God intends.

Love-Based Relating

God's way of relating is love-based. He commands us to relate in this way, and demonstrates it for us. His idea has everything to do with power and control, propulsion and direction. Without power or propulsion we make no progress, and without control or direction we have no intentionality. God has given each person power and control to steward, and a one-flesh couple has the greater advantage.

The other kinds of relating introduced in this chapter are at work in marriages to the extent that a husband and wife are living separate lives, whether opposing or parallel. There is conflict between two opinions of the best use of propulsion and the best use of guidance. The worldly answer is to achieve some kind of balance of power and control. It goes back to that give and take economy instead of the give and receive way of the Kingdom.

Love-based relating chooses instead to harness the power and control to make it obedient to the will of God. The practical application of this is seen in the one-flesh union's ability to combine power from each person and submit it to guidance that agrees with God. This is unstoppable. It makes the godly couple a force to be reckoned with.

We need a good understanding of love from God's perspective. Love is demonstrated by sacrifice; that is to give up something of yourself for the benefit of another person. Jesus commanded that we love one another as He loved us.[15] Then He describes the greatest act of love as being willing to lay down your life for another. It is important to notice that our love is proven by being willing to die, but it is up to God alone whether we live or die. Therefore, this passage is showing us that true love is to willingly sacrifice our personal identity for someone else. Am I willing to give up everything that defines me as me, physically, emotionally and spiritually? That is the hard question of tough love.

The other characteristic of true love is that it operates without coercion or manipulation. It must be an act of free will. Jesus made that kind of choice when He gave His life for us. He said that no one took His life, but He chose to lay it down.[16] His death would not have been an act of love if it had been demanded by the Father or the devil. This is the pattern we must follow, to sacrifice our personal identity for another willingly.

Love-based relating between a husband and wife is modeled after this kind of sacrifice.[17] When a husband loves his wife as Christ loves the church we see love-based relating; we see each person sacrificing self for the benefit of the other. This allows the "we" part of the relationship to grow. Two separate identities become one flesh, and two completely different people think and act like one.

Consider God's superior design idea for marriage that allows us to look through each other's lenses. For example, a picture is a two-dimensional thing having height and width. It lacks depth of field. However, with binocular vision we can see in three dimensions. We are actually seeing two separate images and comparing them. The subtle differences give perspective and fuller understanding. Similarly, when a husband and wife operate as one flesh they can see separate images and compare them for better perspective and fuller understanding.

This process works because the individuals are differentiated; they have different lenses and different points of view. This brings us back to the Trinity picture where separate entities with unique identities are merged into one Person. As a husband and wife, we are distinct and distinguishable, yet we are merged together in oneness. That means we have oneness in purpose with common goals instead of compromised goals. This is imperative for the coordination of direction. It also means we have oneness in intent, by which we coordinate propulsion. The key is to remember our pronouns: emphasize "we, us, and our" over "me, my, you and your."

In love-based relationships we have freedom to be ourselves. God has the authority to override your free will, but He will not. Overriding another person's free will is to be an abuser, and God will not do it. He loves us too much to manipulate, force, coerce or trick us into doing anything against our will. The devil does not have the authority to override our free will, but he will do anything he can to deceive us into giving him that authority. He is an abuser.

Love can only be expressed outside of compulsion. If there is control exercised by one person over another in any part of a relationship, then love cannot be expressed there. But if there is freedom to be yourself, then you are also free to control yourself. That is why Paul instructs us to be devoted in love and honor the other above ourselves.[18] We choose in love to prefer the other, sacrificing from our own rights and privileges for our spouse. We see the multiplication factor of God's character as we outdo one another in showing honor.

Let's review how we overcome the harmful ways of relating to each other with love-based relating.

We overcome using the law to control another by operating in the New Covenant. The Old Covenant was law based and when you broke the law you paid the penalty. It was cause and effect, action and consequence, give and take. In the New Covenant you are saved by grace and made righteous. It is a supernatural transaction performed by God. When you ask for forgiveness, God grants it and you become righteous; not perfect but righteous.

We need to do the same thing in our marriage relationship. We overcome law with grace by extending forgiveness to our spouse and seeing him as righteous; not perfect but righteous. We grant forgiveness instead of holding him to his consequences. We redeem the effect by covering the cause with love. This is God's model that demonstrates how love fulfills the law.

We overcome using shame to control by moving from condemnation to conviction. This is the role of the Holy Spirit, to convict of sin, and He does it without leaving us in a state of guilt and shame. Sometimes the Holy Spirit uses us as a vessel for bringing a word of conviction to the one we love, but only when we are pure enough to carry it. Otherwise, we pollute the message and it comes across as condemnation leading to shame.

Conviction is when the Holy Spirit taps me on the shoulder to get my attention, points out my sin, and offers me an opportunity for redemption. I become aware of my sin by His instruction so that I can choose to do something about it.

Since sin separates the parties of a relationship, this gentle reminder calls it to my attention so I can choose to do something about it.

Condemnation's purpose is to produce shame that acts as a wedge in the relationship, keeping us apart. It comes from the "accuser of the brethren" to shame us. "Do you see what you did? You're worthless. You call yourself a Christian?" These statements are used to keep us in hiding instead of reconciliation.

Forgiveness is cleansing. If you have been struggling under the weight of shame, then ask God for forgiveness. As soon as you know He has forgiven, the shame will disappear. If you have been shamed by your spouse, then ask him for forgiveness. As soon as you know you have been released from the accusation, the shame will disappear. If you have been putting shame on your spouse then forgive him for whatever accusations you have against him. Forgiveness cleanses it. Then ask him to forgive you for promoting a shame-based relationship.

We overcome using needs or lust to control in a relationship by looking to God as our provider. Lust has an unending appetite, and when we look to our spouse to fill our needs there will always be a gap. Our spouse is not able to fill the hole that only God can fill. We must look to God to supply us spiritually, emotionally and physically with everything we need. His resources are always perfect and sufficient when we trust in Him. Test yourself in this, and discover what you consider to be your source.

We learn how to operate in a love-based relationship instead of a need-based relationship by being generous and thankful. This is the antidote to the unending appetite: give it away to convince yourself that you are not dependent on it. A generous attitude always brings a sense of well-being as it builds trust in God. Gratitude is the opposite of lust and can be practiced at any time. Then you will not put unrealistic demands on your spouse or others.

We overcome using fear to control in our relationship by building faith. There is no fear in love, but perfect love casts out fear.[19] Fear has to do with punishment, and punishment is a payment for crime. The opposite of punishment is forgiveness. When we practice forgiveness in our marriage then the risk of punishment is gone, and the basis for fear evaporates as well. This requires that we have faith in our spouse, meaning we believe and trust that we will be forgiven rather than punished.

Consider your immediate reaction to fear and be aware of your native tendency, whether it is to fight or withdraw. The villain personality that would respond aggressively must put his faith in God to overcome fear. He must also trust his spouse rather than try to control her with fear. The victim personality that would respond by withdrawing must put his faith in God to overcome the fear, also. He must trust his spouse to lead toward God and to create a safe environment through which to live in freedom from fear.

Love-based relating allows us to work according to our strengths. Individual strengths complement, and that is why we need to merge our identities. We work best when we operate as one flesh because we maximize each other's gifts and talents. Remember the example of binocular vision, together we can see more dimensions than we can separately.

When I face a tough decision, I want to invoke best thinking. If we assume the average weight of the human brain as a measure of intelligence, then the best thinking I can do on my own is about three pounds. While that is an amazing amount of thought-power, it leaves room for improvement. Better thinking can happen when I add my wife's brain into the formula. Obviously, if we simply trade back and forth between our brains we only access three pounds, though we may alternate between which brain is contributing. But if we are able to think together, to add our brain power, then we can double our thinking capacity.

Best thinking involves three, so let me carry this analogy a step further. In a particularly tough situation, I want to know what my wife thinks because she thinks way differently than I do. We approach problems differently, assess them differently, and look for solutions differently because we have different experiences and strengths. Yet, we are one flesh and have a common goal. I need to know what she thinks. But I also want to know what God thinks. He is the source of wisdom, and wisdom comes from a multiple of advisors as they confirm His truth. When we seek His wisdom together it resolves conflict and overcomes fear, lust, shame and the law.

This is the model of Christ and the church. God designed us as the body of Christ to operate in best thinking together, as one entity. There is no room for manipulating, controlling, giving or taking power, or acting as victims or villains. Each of us are members of the body, created by God as He intended us to be, and in that freedom we are able to operate in love.

When we understand this model as husband and wife, then we can operate in this way as members of the body of Christ. When Christ is the head and He leads us into the Father's will, there is no stopping us. It is maximum power and perfect direction for ultimate impact.

Marriage Rx

Chapter 6

Trust

Friends and Enemies

We often attend retreats at a conference center on the Oregon coast. It is a wonderful facility with two of the buildings situated right along the beach with a full view of the ocean. One is a fairly new structure with three floors and multiple gables that give it a distinctive appearance. It is lovely.

A friend of ours helped build that building. It was from him that we learned a secret that we would never have suspected. The building's foundation is out of plumb from corner to corner by a full three inches. It isn't square. The builders discovered the problem when they tried to frame up the walls and boards came out too short or too long; plywood sheets did not fit properly in the spaces for which they were cut. They learned rather soon in the construction process that everything, from the first to the third floor, had to be measured specifically; they could not trust the measurements of the foundation.

The crew started work with certain assumptions about the foundation, assumptions that were not accurate.

Trust is Foundational

In marriage, trust is foundational. It isn't hard to see why. Consider the definition of trust:

> Assured reliance on the character, ability, strength, or truth of someone of something.

Synonyms for trust are,

> assurance, certainty, certitude, confidence,
> conviction, credence, credit, dependence,
> expectation, faith, gospel truth, home,
> positiveness, reliance, stock, store, sureness.

The greatest injury a relationship can sustain is to the element of trust. As you ponder definitions and synonyms above, think about their opposites. Unreliable. Unable. Weak. Uncertain. Wishy-washy. Undependable. Liar... When such antonyms manifest themselves in a relationship, each person begins to be suspicious of the ability and the behavior of the other; they begin to take steps to defend themselves against failure and hurt.

Real trust is to have confidence in Someone. The Someone is God, and for that reason we use the capitalized form of the pronoun. God is the only one that is completely trustworthy. He is the One that is perfect. It is proper that we trust in Him because He never fails us or forsakes us. [1]

Trust is the very essence of love-based relating, as we explored in the previous chapter. God is love. We love each other because He first loved us. [2] When we love each other we are expressing the pure character of God. Love and trust go hand in hand, and together they overcome fear. As the scripture says, there is no fear in love. Just as love builds trust, fear destroys it.

There is a form of real trust that can occur between humans, even though they are not God. In this case one person can trust the reflection of God being displayed in another person. We are created in His image and are able to reflect His perfect character. When we put our trust in others, real trust happens because we trust the character of God being reflected in them. We cannot trust their sin nature, because sinfulness is not trustworthy.

We cannot force ourselves to trust any more than we can force ourselves to have faith. Faith is to know for sure that something is true; it is not faith to believe in something that is not true. Similarly, trust is to believe in the character of God; it is not trust to believe in anything less than that. *Trust* and *expect* are not synonyms, though they are sometimes used interchangeably in common language. The statement "you can trust a liar to lie" is better phrased "you can expect a liar to lie." Real trust is an expectation in which we can place our confidence, and that is why it must match the perfect character of God.

It is impossible for any person to perfectly reflect the character of God in this sinful world, so it is impossible to be perfectly trustworthy. Instead, trustworthiness is determined by dependability, and dependability is measured by how accurately and consistently one depicts God's nature.

Maybe you can think of someone that acts a certain way around one group but in another setting is completely different. That person does not have consistent character. It makes you wonder which persona is real and which is phony, and this ambiguity leads to distrust.

We say that people are acting "out of character" when they are not being themselves. It is better to say that people are acting out of character when they are not being a true reflection of God. In both cases, acting out of character is sin because we were created in God's image. In the chapter on forgiveness and reconciliation, we learned that we cannot be reconciled to the sin nature. Now we see that we cannot trust it either. This is important to understand.

We were ministering to a couple that suffered from broken trust. The husband had destroyed trust by committing adultery. The wife wanted to trust him again because she knew a marriage could not thrive without it, but she could not. She was trying to trust his character, but it was the same character that had failed her. It is impossible to trust the sin nature. She can only grant trust again by putting prophetic confidence in his redeemed identity.

This redeemed identity is the result of Christ's saving work on the cross by which the person is a new creation,[3] accurately reflecting God's character. We must claim it prophetically because it is yet to be evidenced or completed, though it is as good as done according to His promise. Just as God sees past our sinful nature through Calvary, our trust is placed in our spouse's perfected character.

When a husband and wife put prophetic confidence in each other's redeemed identity they help each other grow in Christ-likeness. God put us together to affect one another, and by reflecting each other's character it helps us work out our salvation until we become blameless and innocent children of God.[4] That is why we must be see each other according to the redeemed identity.

Trust is first learned in childhood, as it says in Psalms: "You made me trust You at my mother's breasts."[5] This is the Psalm that Jesus quoted while hanging from the cross, and it incredibly describes the agony He was going through. If there were a situation in which trust would be forever broken, this would have been it. Yet, Jesus continued to trust in God just as He had learned to do from infancy.

The responsibilities of an infant are few. When they are first born they need to learn to be content, to live in peace or *shalom*.[6] It is the responsibility of the parents to help them do so. When they are not in peace, usually signaled by crying, the parents take some action to return them to that place of contentment. As they experience this peace, the child begins to build confidence. They are learning to trust their parents.

Trials happen, such as dirty diapers and hunger, and disrupt the infant's peace, but the parenting community helps them return to *shalom* by cleaning them up, feeding them, burping them, and a host of other simple duties. The baby begins to grow up with confidence that these disruptions are temporary and solutions are available.

As a child matures his trials increase and discomforts are more severe. For instance, the bumps and bruises of a toddler turn into injuries as a child, possibly even broken bones. The mature adult faces trials in the physical, emotional and spiritual realms.

Our capacity for enduring trials increases with our success over greater and greater trials. At first the trial may shake us, but we rely on our community to help us overcome until we return to peace. As we experience this, we come to understand that we are unshakable. That is what trust is: being unshakable. Each of us should be mature enough by now that we can return from being hungry to contentment, and even have great confidence that we will be happy again.

Trust finds expression in the present tense. That means it is happening as it is being expressed, not carried over from the past nor awaiting a future condition. Trust hopes in the future, meaning that when we trust our spouse we hope for his or her preferable future. Trust has faith in the person, specifically we trust the character of God being displayed in our spouse.

Trust is redeemed by reconciling the past. If acting in character means I am demonstrating the character of God, and sin is when I'm acting out of character, then my sin nature must be reconciled before trust can be restored. The key step is forgiveness, which we talked about in chapter four. Being forgiven redeems character as the one forgiven becomes a new creation in Christ Jesus. As he or she lives out their identity in Christ, they become trustworthy in the present with a hope for the future.

Real trust is to be at peace in a relationship. The Hebrew word *shalom* is often translated as peace, but it means so much more. It includes the ideas of contentedness, joy, being full, prosperous, blessed, and happy. Certainly peace is recognized by an absence of conflict, such as distrust and suspicion, but it must also be demonstrated on the positive side with this expanded understanding of *shalom*. When a husband and wife are living in mutual trust they are experiencing this deep sense of peace and well-being.

Real trust is a result of a healthy relationship. It is a very predictable outcome for a husband and wife who live as one flesh, are bound by a covenant, willing to be naked and unashamed, are reconciled through forgiveness, and are guided by love-based relating. That is why we covered those topics in the preceding chapters; they are foundational to trust.

True love is the deep desire to know and to be known. Fear and suspicion put one person on the defensive against another and then hiding strategies and unhealthy ways of relating separate them spiritually, emotionally and physically. When the barriers are taken down and each is willing to risk their self-interest for the sake of oneness, peace can return. It is imperative that we learn to return to this place of peace, even as adults. That is where we will find real trust.

One of our favorite translations of the Hebrew word, Shalom, is "well-being." When our shalom (peace) is threatened, it is our well-being that is at stake. This is why trust is so vital in our relationships. Trust brings a quality of well-being into the home; of confidence and assurance.

Furthermore, wrapped up in the idea of peace is the idea of rest. Trust is the ability to rest with someone, and in the case of the Lord, it is the ability to rest *in* Him—the Bible calls it Abiding in Him. When we are unable to give trust, or when trust is broken, our sense of shalom evaporates.

Nobody sets out to break trust. On the contrary, most of us want to extend trust to others and to be trusted ourselves. Why? Because it provides an environment of safety where we can properly give ourselves to the marriage covenant to which we have become a party. We want to trust.

Nevertheless, there are barriers—opponents—to trust in our relationships. Trust is under siege.

Identifying the Enemy

When trust begins to break down, there come feelings of agitation and anxiety. Fear begins to mount. When this happens, we tend to release ourselves to use strategies that we may have abandoned long ago to try to bring control back into our lives, to try to regain a sense of well-being.

But we may not be talking about marriage here. There are other ways that mistrust and fear may creep into our lives—through friends, or another family member. We may even feel backed into a corner by our own children. Wherever trust is violated, fear may enter in and, from within our own hearts, become our enemy. Don't discount this discussion merely because your marriage is built on trust.

Over the last few years we've become aware of many people that are navigating through life with a pervasive sense of *fear and anxiety*. The more we observe this, the more apparent it is that trust and well-being cannot be experienced unless these twin enemies are addressed. The reason is simple. If someone in a relationship lives with anxiety, they find it difficult to trust, and where there is mistrust, suspicion becomes the dominant emotion. Suspicion is a substitute—a poor one—for discernment, and becomes the motivation for accusation and condemnation. Moreover, a husband or wife may not realize that they, themselves, are motivated by fear and so project that fear onto others, making it the central issue of the relationship. Until the fearful one takes ownership of their own emotions, the marriage will be held hostage by a level of mistrust and suspicion.

Sometime ago, Jody awakened to a sense of anxiety and fear. She arrived at the church carrying that anxiousness, but realizing that those feelings were not normal for her. As she sat with some of the ladies who were present at the gathering, she voiced those thoughts. In the discussion that followed, many of the women declared that fear and anxiety *were normal for them.* The feelings were so common for them that they had grown used to them. Fear and anxiety were like elevator music, constantly playing in the background needing to be ignored in order to preserve something like normalcy.

From that experience and others like it, we've come to understand that fear and anxiety are often the result of being hurt in past relationships. They are like sentries—emotional guards—that we unwittingly call upon to prevent future hurts. The result of their presence is that we become hyper-vigilant to threats to our emotional well-being, ready to suspect, accuse and reject anything that might hurt us again. The problem with that is neither of these guards reflect the trustworthy nature of God. Instead, they are tools of darkness that we are trusting—the enemy's henchmen—to protect and care for our soul. The result is that they exert control to the extent that we are unable to rest in our relationships, both in our marriage and elsewhere.

So, what is *fear*? The definition is,

> ...a distressing emotion aroused by impending danger, evil or pain, whether the threat is real or imagined. Often caused by anticipation or

awareness of danger resulting in an overwhelming
urge to flee or freeze.

Note that physical symptoms, amplified by recollected fear, become exaggerated. We can merely think about a past fear and feel heightened anxiety, quickening heart rate or breathing. Moreover, remembering fearful or injurious events can cause us to have a reaction that closely parallels the original feelings, like a flashback—we can re-sense those original fears. Such feelings are called "resentment" and they are another assault on trust in relationship.

The fact is, most of us do what we can to avoid fearful situations. Jody confesses to having an informal list of ways that she does not have to die! On that list are such things as sky-diving, white water rafting and mountain climbing. She acknowledges that she has what she believes to be a healthy fear of those things; therefore she intends to avoid them...always. In matters of sky-diving and bull-riding, she plans on intentionally respecting her fear and staying out of those circumstances.

Sometimes we decide to avoid fearful circumstances unintentionally. In fact, it is possible to react to conditions that we don't consciously even know we're anxious about. Those sentries of fear and anxiety step between us and others protecting us from imaginary fears, but effectively undermining our relationships. It may happen this way: someone approaches you unexpectedly—your spouse or a friend. Something about the situation triggers a feeling that originated at some other time and some other place. Whatever the original situation was, it left it's mark in the form of fear and anxiety so that now, in this new and unrelated situation, the emotions replay and the feelings reemerge.

Dan remembers a situation in a local restaurant where two friends, a married couple, came in and were seated at a booth across the dining room. When he saw them, he made a mental note to greet them before he left. A few minutes later, after he finished his appointment, he strolled across the room to say hello. As he approached the booth where his friends were seated the woman glanced up in surprise and immediately registered an expression of extreme terror, a grimace that would have been more appropriate if she had looked up to see a knife-wielding assailant rushing toward her. Why? Apparently, Dan's unanticipated presence had triggered some reflexive response drawn from a past experience. Fear and anxiety, those dark sentries, had taken up their post in the woman's life and infected her relationships with fear and suspicion, an infection that was, even then, threatening her marriage.

This experience suggests that fear may be more than just an emotion. Scripture teaches that there is such a thing as a "spirit of fear" and that its outcome is something like slavery. [7] We are of the opinion that fear of this kind is a tool of the enemy and that when we are caught in that cycle of fear we are restrained to the point of impotence in our walk of faith. It causes us to be tied like slaves to past experiences and the resentment that they arouse in us. That is why counseling sometimes fails to break through the alienation that some couples experience. Both parties may be satisfied that the counsel they are receiving is wise and appropriate, yet the fear that is camped between the two—fear of further pain and abuse—prevents them from trusting one another.

Ingredients of Fear

What are the ingredients of fear? What allows fear to remain between a husband and a wife; between parents and their children? What gives fear the ability to operate? When does it show up in our lives, forcing us to confront it?

Fear remains hidden until an event brings it to light and triggers emotions related to a past experience, then it emerges from the shadows of our lives. We face a new situation that has some components that are similar to a past event—we may not even know which one—and suddenly, without warning, we experience feelings that seem out of step with the moment. We feel more intensely than seems warranted.

For example, a wife, when she was very young, has been wounded by a thoughtless comment from one of her parents. She doesn't think about it much. Oh, occasionally that unpleasant encounter comes to mind, but not often and she doesn't dwell on it because it's over and done—that was a long time ago. Then she is having a discussion with her husband. They are working through the subject of their concern. They are communicating effectively and making progress on a decision. Then he makes a comment using a tone of voice that causes her to react. She may not even be aware of what has happened; that the tone he used was an echo of the words that had caused so much pain for her when she was a little girl. Suddenly, the conversation takes an abrupt, unexpected negative turn. Where there had been productive dialog, she begins to become defensive and withdraw from the subject. Fear had found a foothold and come into the relationship as the wife experiences the present conversation twice—once in the moment, and once in a moment a long time ago—effectively multiplying her feelings times two.

Fear also shows up when there is an unknown, seemingly unpredictable, future. Imagine how the sudden loss of employment might affect a family of four. Have you ever had something like that happen? Most of us have. We are going confidently through life, trusting our circumstances, when— wham!—there is a downturn in the economy; we or one of our children get sick; there is an accident, or we get transferred out of state. The future becomes foggy and uncertain. Fear creeps—no, leaps—into our lives. In short, what we don't know, we can't control, and that makes us fearful because we are under the mistaken impression that we can control things. Under those conditions, we find it impossible to rest and we get whipped into a cycle of fear and anxiety that gives room for the enemy to function in our circumstances.

This cycle often begins when we allow ourselves to engage in "futile speculations." Here's what the apostle Paul said about that:

> We are destroying speculations and every lofty thing raised up against the knowledge of God, and we are taking every thought captive to the obedience of Christ... [8]

We are to destroy speculations and lofty thoughts. These are false notions that argue we ought to have control over things that, in reality, are beyond us. The appropriate posture is to yield our circumstances to God.

There is a book that has been published—perhaps you've seen it at the local bookstore—titled, *The Worst Case Scenario Survival Handbook.*[9] The book is a gallery of nightmare scenarios and unlikely events, complete with instructions on how to handle each improbable situation should it occur. The result is entertaining. Not so entertaining is when we find ourselves playing that same game in our mind. Jody confesses to creating a mental gallery of her own "worst case scenarios" and a litany of 'what ifs' in an effort to outthink her circumstances before disaster struck. In effect, she was creating a fear response long before a real circumstance came along that might even justify such a response. She's probably not the only one to play the "worst case scenario" game.

The problem with that kind of mental exercise is that it wastes a lot of time that should be spent learning to trust God in our circumstances. It is difficult to cultivate trust when the seeds of fear are already rooted in our soul. Trying to outthink an unknown future amounts to a mind full of renegade thoughts attempting to elude capture by the Lord, which falls into the category of speculation.

This is not to say that fear is never justified. Indeed, few would blame us if we admitted to being afraid of a rattlesnake or of a charged power line dangling from a pole after a storm. Such circumstances have two qualities that are present simultaneously: the danger is imminent and potent. As you read this, it is likely you are not actively afraid of these things because neither of them is nearby—the danger is not imminent even though the danger in them is potent. On the other hand, sometimes we are afraid of things that are imminent but are not potent. We are larger than a spider and, presumably, could use the size of our shoe to advantage should we encounter one. Nevertheless, many of us regard a spider crawling on us as potent enough to justify fear.

Fear is designed to protect us from harm when facing imminent and potent danger. If those qualities are not present, then fear becomes an obstacle. When we are exposed to certain thoughts over time, negative assessments of our ability or appearance for example, our self-image and confidence can erode. After hearing those negative thoughts over and over again, we begin to worry—another word for, 'fear'—that these things really are true. We become afraid of what we will never be; afraid of failure and rejection. What happens is that we begin to accept a different destiny for ourselves than the one God has for us. Rather than step into our God-given future, we begin to walk into a dark destiny that is crafted to neutralize our confidence in the love of others. After all, how can others truly love us when we are convinced in our hearts that we are unlovely? The result is that a husband who genuinely loves his wife may find her to be distant and unresponsive. Why? She believes herself to be unlovable, making it difficult to accept that anyone, even her husband, can find any value in her. That same fear may limit her ability to trust the love of God. Speculations have been raised up against the knowledge of God.

Thought patterns like this create a deep rut in our heart that often makes it difficult for us to accept that the promises of the Bible can be true for us. Ask yourself, as you consider some of the miracles of scripture, whether you can accept what you read or are you inclined to doubt that they can be applied to you. Many of us never get around to interrogating those doubts. We merely accept them and they become secret thoughts that we carry with us and believe. Often such patterns are part of our heritage from previous generations. Grandparents were worriers. So were parents. That is just the way things are.

That is an example of what is called "a spiritual foothold," a generational pattern that is assumed to be unchangeable. Tragically, many Christians live with footholds, forgetting that God has called us to a different destiny, one that is not framed in fear, but released in freedom. In order to live into that freedom we have to recognize fearful thoughts in their many disguises and interrogate them; that is, determine their source and deliberately choose to live outside them.

At their core, fearful thoughts are rooted in the idea that love ends. Consider the words of the book of Hebrews:

> Since therefore the children share in flesh and blood, He Himself likewise partook of the same things, that through death He might destroy the one who has the power of death, that is, the devil, and deliver all those who through fear of death were subject to lifelong slavery. [10]

God has declared His love to be eternal. By sending Jesus as the grace-gift to draw us to Himself, he opened the gate to an eternal relationship with Him. Fear and anxiety declare the opposite. They argue that love can be lost, rejected or forgotten. The apostle John stated that "perfect love casts out fear" indicating that the two are mutually exclusive. They cannot coexist. The problem is, many of us live with fear which stands as an obstacle to God's perfect love.

So, how have we been managing our lives while all that fear has been gouging deep ruts in our heart? The answer is summed up in one word: control. Control is a substitute for genuine trust. It's what happens when one partner tries to place requirements on the behavior in a relationship in order to feel reassured that their fears are unfounded. Of course, placing a few demands on a spouse, child, friend or loved one isn't trusting them; it is trusting the demands.

Anxiety

What's the difference between fear and anxiety? They are close cousins but they are different in that anxiety is the internalization of fear, which prevents us from entering into rest on a matter. Worry and anxiety are impotent substitutes for prayer. George Mueller, the British evangelist and founder of numerous orphanages across 19th century England said, "The beginning of anxiety is the end of faith and the end of faith is the beginning of anxiety." Worry and anxiety often manifest in a tendency to turn to others (in a marriage, usually our spouse) for something only the Lord can provide. We can only learn trust by focusing on a perfect trust first. This trust in God only happens if we believe He is good.

The practice of thanksgiving and gratitude develops our trust and reinforces our understanding of God's goodness. In a previous chapter, we described a person's life as a cup that needs to be filled by parents. Many of us emerge from childhood with less in our "cup" than is needed; moreover, some of what we lack is the result of wounds that we sustained while growing up. These become the basis for fear, worry and anxiety.

The Ring of Woundedness

Jody has used the diagram below as a tool in counseling to help people, individuals as well as couples, identify the source of problems that they face in life. The outer ring is for listing issues that are of concern, things that a person or couple might identify as threatening their well being or unity. These are issues in a relationship that might cause a couple to

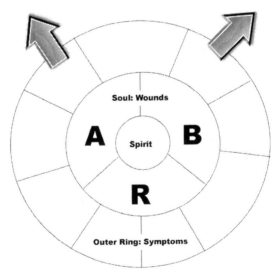

B ~ Betrayal
A ~ Abandonmnent
R ~ Rejection

consider seeing a counselor together. Depression might appear in that outer ring, infidelity or even excessive spending. In other words, the outer ring contains a list of symptoms that have appeared in the couple's life; patterns of behavior that have become a disruption to unity in the marriage because they are more than just feelings, they are expressed outwardly and have influenced decisions that impact others.

The next ring in is the region of our soul—mind, will and emotions—and this is the area of our life where we can easily be wounded. Many have been wounded repeatedly and deeply at the level of the soul. Those wounds are the result of three things: betrayal, abandonment and rejection.

Betrayal means to deliver or expose to the power of an enemy by treachery or disloyalty; to prove false to; to disappoint the hopes or expectations of someone; to deceive, mislead or seduce; to reveal or expose in violation of confidence. Betrayal says, "I'll sacrifice you on my behalf." Or, "Me first, no matter what it costs you." Some of us have experienced this while growing up or through repeated relationships over the course of our lives. Some of us have even experienced it in marriage. No matter where you have encountered betrayal these symptoms are likely to show up in the outer circle of the diagram:

- Anger.
- Aggressiveness.
- Bitterness.
- Retaliation.
- Self-protection, like maintaining a facade or building emotional walls.
- Pessimism.

Betrayal is the basis *for virtually all* mistrust.

What about *abandonment*? Remember, feelings of abandonment can come from a number of different experiences, like a death in the family, divorce, substance abuse, even job transfer or military deployment. Regardless of how abandonment happens, it can, years later, interrupt a marriage relationship as fears of desertion or being given up or lost pop up unexpectedly. The feelings, though not justified by present circumstances, hearken back to conclusions drawn in the past. The voice of abandonment whispers, "You are not worth staying for. Nobody has a shared covenant with you. At any moment, you will discover how really alone you are..."

When those feelings work into a marriage relationship, symptoms of the dysfunction begin to manifest in that outer ring. Defensive detachment, deep anxiety, jealousy, despair and a kind of childish anguish that reacts to circumstances with anger begin to appear if the experience of abandonment is not healed.

Finally, *rejection*. This wound is defined as, "to cast off or discard as being found worthless or unsatisfactory." It doesn't take much imagination to empathize with such feelings. Nobody wants to think of themselves as worthless or unsatisfactory. This is how it works out in relationship: "Unless you please me, I'll withhold approval and acceptance. I don't respect you. You are of no value and are not appreciated."

Various kinds of body language are also common to rejection. Among them are outbursts of anger, disgusted looks, impatient answers or questions, and isolation, that is, withdrawing in an attempt to control another person.

The symptoms of rejection that appear in that outer ring include self-hatred, loneliness, self-pity, seeking affirmation and validation in unhealthy ways, what the Bible calls "being a man-pleaser." When forgiveness is needed in a relationship, someone who has been wounded by rejection has difficulty feeling forgiven or offering forgiveness. After all, they are rejected, or so they think. They are not worthy of forgiveness, neither should others be forgiven, because rejection is the ultimate punishment for failure in their mind. Such people are often judgmental, critical, angry, resentful and sarcastic—all ways of rejecting. People wounded by rejection are often easily manipulated. Why? Because they wish they could reverse the feelings of rejection by doing things that will assure acceptance.

Wounds and Infection

Wounds in our past—betrayal, abandonment, rejection—can set us up for an infection in our soul.

Think of an injury left untreated and unhealed. Without treatment, it becomes dangerous and painful, needing to be drained, cleansed and bandaged. The infection can actually be fatal if left alone. In our soul, an injury behaves similarly, in that it is tender and vulnerable to being "bumped" by circumstances—triggered. When that happens, imagine arrows coming from that inner circle (the wounds: betrayal, abandonment and rejection) and penetrating that outer circle of symptoms. The problem with many counseling efforts is that it attempts to treat the symptoms in that outer circle without first cleansing the wounds of the soul. All that accomplishes is a diversion from the core issue. Counselors will report that clients who are suicidal will often turn their destructive tendencies toward behaviors that are self-destructive even though they are not imminently so. A person with an eating disorder or other addiction, may turn to some other behavior when they attempt to deal with food issues. They may let their spending get out of control, or become obsessed with some other behavior. The reason that treatment of the symptoms diverts behavior rather than makes fundamental changes is that the wound has not been identified, confessed and dealt with in a manner that replaces the injury with the truth of God's love, healing and forgiveness. In effect, the inner circle is fueling the outer ring of symptoms.

This is why we need to turn further inward, toward the center of the diagram, which is that place in us that is called our spirit. This is the deep place that God's Holy Spirit longs to enter so He can abide with us and in us.

The condition of abiding is sometimes interrupted because our wounds and their consequences are not exclusively aimed outward toward other people; often they are aimed at the Lord. The result is that many have difficulty accepting *the Lord is good.* If the Spirit is to find an abiding place in the core of a person's being—the heart—then His goodness needs to be acknowledged and trusted. That knowledge is the key to releasing the Lord to address the wounded places that motivate wrong responses to others and disrupt relationships that are supposed to reflect the reliability and fullness of God. Without the release of the Spirit, then fear is allowed to rise up within us—an infection. If the Spirit is permitted to remove the power of fear, which is the basis of unhealed wounds, then restoration and healing can begin and the outer behavior can be transformed. Moreover, fear is not permitted to occupy the throne of our life; instead we invite the Lord that we are trusting to operate His will through us.

When Trust is Broken

The result of betrayal, abandonment and rejection can make it difficult to trust or, when the perceptions of the circumstances within a marriage are filtered through our wounds, difficult to be trusted. The erosion of trust in a marriage doesn't need to be the result of a catastrophe or big event; it can begin in a hundred small ways based on our personal perceptions. Regardless of how trust is broken or challenged in our marriage, there are consequences.

George MacDonald said, "It is a greater compliment to be trusted than to be loved." Isn't that a remarkable statement? While we all want to be loved, there is something special about being trusted. If a friend confides in you, trusting you with a secret or a private need, it says something about your relationship with that person. It is humbling to know that you are trusted and relied upon to receive the information and guard it.

Trust in a relationship is much like a window. It is the glass through which we see one another. Dan has a backyard office with French doors looking out into the yard. While he was preparing to teach about trust, he noticed that the glass in the doors had not been cleaned for what looked like a very long time. Although he could see through the glass, the view was definitely not what it could be. He made a note to wash the windows as soon as he could. Indeed, once they had been washed, he was amazed at how much brighter his office seemed!

There are three "trust-busters" in a relationship. First, there may be a catastrophic breech of trust, like unfaithfulness, abandonment or gross dishonesty. Secondly, trust may be withheld for reasons that have little to do with the one who is mistrusted, that is a husband or wife may refuse to place confidence in their partner because of fear born from a previous painful experience of betrayal, abandonment or rejection. Finally, trust can erode due to carelessness. In a dozen small ways a person may communicate that he or she does not care about the well-being of the other—a disregard for the covenant, which is the promise that each party will act selflessly.

Sadly, it's fairly common for trust to get bruised due to carelessness. Most of us have gotten careless ourselves or have been offended by the carelessness of another. We hear ourselves say, "well, nobody is perfect." and we mean it. We know very well that we're going to make a mistake, and we expect that our partner will, too. So, why are we surprised and offended when it happens? Furthermore, what is the outcome when we feel trust has been violated?

Often, when trust is violated, couples may slip into shame-based relating. The husband is careless and misses an appointment...again; the wife becomes judgmental and steps back from the relationship leaving the husband to feel untrustworthy. For his part, the husband becomes defensive and begins waiting for his wife to make a mistake so he can deflect her judgment back upon her. The result is emotional distance between husband and wife that becomes habitual— since I can't trust you, I guess I'll just have to take care of myself. If, as George McDonald said, trust is a compliment, then trust withheld has an opposite effect. It is something of an insult.

In the end, eroded trust pushes us toward isolation and, ultimately, selfishness. Even if you feel thoroughly justified in taking care of yourself because you don't trust your spouse to uphold the covenant, the result is the same: you become self-centered as you keep a sharp lookout for your own needs. Or, if you find yourself trying to earn back the trust of someone who is judging you as untrustworthy, then you are effectively "looking in the mirror" all of the time in an effort to determine whether you are measuring up. In either case, it's all about you, and either way, it is the covenant relationship that suffers.

In covenant terms, it is the husband's responsibility to care for the needs of his bride. Conversely, it is the wife who takes responsibility for the needs of her husband. The husband assumes unlimited responsibility for the wife; the wife takes unlimited responsibility for the husband. The husband assumes unlimited liability for his wife; the wife takes unlimited liability for her husband. As a couple does those things, they draw closer together in a way that actually demonstrates the love and character of God. To the extent that either turns away from the other, that is the extent to which the covenant relationship is weakened and the image of God's covenant with His creation is spoiled.

Let's imagine how this may work out in a marriage.

Let's say a couple, George and Emily, are making just enough money every month to pay their bills, but not much more. Emily hears a funny noise in the family car and calls it to George's attention. George is no mechanic, but knows enough to diagnose the problem and decides to fix it himself to save some money. Emily is relieved that it won't be as expensive as she feared, even if she has some private doubts about George's ability.

George goes to the auto parts store and buys the part and sets to work. He doesn't discover that he has bought the wrong part until he damages it trying to fit it into place. Now, a job that was going to cost one amount is going to cost over twice that because of the damaged part.

George tells Emily what happened. He feels awful about the mistake and says so. Emily responds with frustration: "I thought you said you knew how to fix it." "I do," George responds, lamely, "but they gave me the wrong part..."

Suddenly, the car isn't the only thing that needs fixing. George, who felt bad about the mistake already, goes away from the conversation feeling even worse. As he goes back to work on the car, he makes a mental vow not to tell Emily the next time he makes a mistake of this kind. Meanwhile, Emily is thinking that she was right all along when she doubted that her husband could fix the car, and that next time she wouldn't be so foolish as to trust him to be able to do what he said he could. Instead, she would mention it to the neighbor who is a competent back yard mechanic.

Without knowing it, George and Emily have stopped trusting each other in subtle ways. He has privately come to fear being judged as incapable, and she has begun to feel vulnerable because George cannot care for her.

The window through which they see each other is dirty. They have ceased to see one another with the eyes of trust, and though the incident is minor—this isn't a catastrophic breach of trust—it can begin to undermine their relationship if left unchecked.

Perhaps Emily's doubt about her husband's ability becomes an invitation to imagine what it might be like to be married to a more capable man. Or, maybe she begins to doubt George's truthfulness, wondering if he isn't a bit too proud for his own good. Her doubts seem more significant as she notices other mistakes he has made.

George, on the other hand, begins to wonder if Emily understands him. He feels unappreciated and judged. He begins to wonder if there are women who might value him more than the one he married. As the resentment builds, he allows himself to compare Emily to other women he knows.

Broken trust, even if the event that causes it seems minor, can have a far reaching effect, especially if past wounds amplify present experience. A man who defends himself from his wife with distance may turn to pornography, which is a two-dimensional experience that does not require communication. It is a selfish occupation that rejects relationship and covenant. A woman who feels vulnerable and unloved may find validation in daydreams, stories of forbidden romance or even "innocent" flirtations, activities that don't require committed relationship and covenant. Such private escapes are attempts to bandage damaged trust.

But private thoughts can cease to be private and start to involve others outside the marriage. Hidden fantasy can open the door to an "emotional affair," that is a relationship with a specific person, like a co-worker or an internet acquaintance. Casual conversation or contact via email, text message or chat room can begin to fulfill a need for intimacy. It can be said of such relationships that, "nothing happened. It's just a friendship." But a friendship that takes the place of conversational intimacy within the marriage is a step toward infidelity—an affair—one of those catastrophic breaches of trust that effectively becomes a rock hurled through the window of relationship.

Taking Action

Broken trust is an injury. It needs to be dealt with. It needs to be tended to before it becomes infected and begins to compromise other dimensions of the relationship. As covenant people we are called upon to be constantly vigilant to "preserve the unity in the bond of peace,"[11] most importantly in the context of marriage. When we find ourselves doubting the trust we have in each other, we need to identify the incident and treat it as a threat to unity.

Friedrich Nietzsche said, "I am not upset that you lied to me. I am upset that from now on I cannot believe you." His words resonate with our experience. When we catch someone in a lie, we are reluctant to believe future words. We say, "Fool me once, shame on you. Fool me twice, shame on me." In reality, though, Nietzsche's statement is false because trust is not something that we earn to begin with. Like God's grace, it is something that is given to us. Trust is assumed at the beginning of a relationship. It is that spotless glass window through which we see one another. But as we go through the process of living together our confidence can get bruised—and usually does. At that point trust stops being an assumption and becomes a decision, an intentional choice to preserve the unity in the bond of peace; to extend to our partner the compliment of trust. Choosing the path of trust is one of the greatest challenges of married life, but it is also one of the greatest demonstrations of the power of covenant.

Restoring Trust

The word fidelity comes from the Latin *fidelis* that means faithfulness. It has the connotation of a person being faithful to another, but can also mean faithfulness to one's self. We have looked at this second shade of meaning already, that trustworthiness is based on how faithfully we reflect the character of God. In a marriage, trustworthiness is also based on how faithfully we maintain our covenant.

Infidelity is often considered to be synonymous with adultery. By definition, it is a lack of faith or constancy, especially with regard to sexual faithfulness; but it is also any act or instance of disloyalty. For purposes of restoring trust we will consider infidelity to be physical or emotional adultery as well as any untrustworthy behavior regarding finances, honesty, safety, or other core values. Infidelity leads to broken trust.

Distrust that is brought into a marriage is projected into the union. For example, if the husband has a broken understanding of trust because of a failed first marriage or distrust in his family of origin, he will project distrust on his wife. However, if trust is broken inside the marriage it is reflected in the union. That means if the husband does something untrustworthy then the wife will reflect that lack of trust to him, as he does to her. To be dealt with, distrust must be traced back to its roots.

Trust cannot be earned. It must be granted. This is the most important principle about restoring trust in a relationship. It is given by the free will of the one extending trust to the other as a beneficiary of that trust. If you have done something to destroy the trust in your relationship there is nothing you can do to earn it back. There is no amount of time that will reconcile it, no heroic feats will compensate, and no promise of changed behavior that will carry the day. Broken trust remains broken until it is granted by the injured party.

This is bad news for the culprit because it is completely outside his or her control to restore trust, no matter how much they want it. This is also bad news for the victim, because trust can only be restored by an act of somebody else's will, when he or she chooses to grant it. In either case, no amount of time or effort will change the broken trust. However, there is good news. Once you accept the fact that trust cannot be earned, it opens the way for it to be granted. To grant trust is a gift of love that allows a couple to move toward a hopeful future together. However, it is not effective to simply grant trust while ignoring the breach that caused distrust to begin with. Distrust comes as a result of real offense.

One woman came for prayer because she felt so betrayed by her husband's affair. She said: "I keep wondering if I'm being foolish. I feel like I'd be a fool to allow this to happen to me again. I've felt so foolish from all of this and I don't want to be a fool again."

When you offer someone your gift of love, forgiveness and trust, it is only reasonable to hope that they will treasure that gift. When he refuses or rejects your gift of love, despises it, and treats it with disrespect, that is painful. But if he treats your gift that way, you are not the one being a fool.

It is not foolish to offer the gift of love to someone. We all want to be loved, and when we offer our love we hope for reciprocity. We hope to be loved in return. Just as we all want to be loved, we really want to be free to love. This is true because we are created in God's image, and we are designed to love. When we love we are acting the most like God, and He loved us while we were rejecting Him.[12] It is painful to us to be constrained from loving because it is against our nature to be so restricted. In cases of distrust there are two sources of pain: first is the conflict in the relationship expressed as rejection, abandonment and betrayal; second is the conflict of not being able to express love.

Restoring trust must be a common goal. Trust cannot be built or maintained by one person only, it requires agreement. That is the main reason this topic is covered in the sixth chapter. It is built on the premise that a man is joined to his wife and they become one flesh.[13] It requires a promise or covenant that locks this agreement in place. It operates in an environment where each is able to be naked and unashamed with the other, know how to forgive one another, to be reconciled, and living in a love-based relationship. With these tools, a couple can experience trust as an integral part of their commitment to a merged life together.

If trust has not been part of your relationship in the past because your marriage could not support it, you can be encouraged that trust can be supported by your marriage now and in the future. Restored trust is an expectation that will manifest in the future. It cannot be created in the past, nor does it require a revision of history. As stated before, it is that prophetic confidence in our redeemed character.

There are two important building blocks to restored trust. Faith is the conviction of things that are not seen and the assurance of what we hope for,[14] and hope is the confident expectation of a preferable future. Trust rests on these two.

True faith is to believe in something because it is true. It is not true faith to believe in something that is false in an attempt to make it true. That is nonsense. In other words, it is nonsense to believe in your spouse's character based on past experience or marital performance. Everyone sins and is tempted, and it is foolishness to put your faith in the willpower of anyone's ability to resist sin.[15] We will not restore trust for long if we put our faith in our spouse's will power. Our confidence must be placed in that person's ability to reflect the character and likeness of God. With our faith in the redeeming power of God, we can have hope in a better future. Even if our past has been compromised by sin and broken promises, we can have confidence in the future. That is where hope is to be found.

Practical Steps to Restore Trust

- Identify the breach of trust.
- Create a safe environment for discussion.
- Share your concern: I saw, I thought, I believed.
- Interrogate the belief: Could you help me with my conclusion?
- Participate in active listening.
- The goal is truth.

Trust is broken by suspicion of disloyalty. The breach of trust is the action, event or attitude that caused suspicion. The first step is to identify the source of the breach by asking what thing or things set off the suspicion. This is done without accusation, judgment or condemnation to protect faith and hope as the foundation for trust.

It is possible that suspicions arise from within a person, and they are treated individually. For instance, a jealous man admitted that he did not trust his wife. When we tried to identify which of her attitudes or actions caused this breach of trust he could not name one. He had always felt suspicious. We went to prayer and asked God to reveal the source of these feelings. God showed him that he believed he was worthless and he feared that his wife was unsatisfied with him. When this man got a glimpse of his value from God's perspective it immediately took away his fear and the accompanying suspicions. His trust was restored in his wife.

It is possible that suspicions arise in the relationship, and they are treated jointly. This sets up the second step, to create a safe environment for discussion. If you do not already have an agreed-upon strategy for establishing a safe environment then you should review that part of the third chapter, Naked and Unashamed. Prepare for a serious conversation, allowing enough time without interruptions or distractions, where each of you will be at the top of your game. Remember the acronym "HALT" and don't start this if someone is hungry, angry, lonely or tired. Creating a safe environment for one another reduces the chances that this topic will drive you apart instead of together.

In this safe environment you are ready to take the third step: share your concern. Remember how the mind works for making decisions and beliefs. First, you observe something. Observation is objective and value neutral; it is neither good nor bad. Then you interpret that information by comparing it to what you already know and feel. Finally, you draw a conclusion based on your frame of reference, and this conclusion is your belief. With this in mind, you want to share your concern without judgment or accusation. That means you have to hold your conclusion lightly, willing to let it go upon further scrutiny.

Use this as a pattern for introducing the breach: "I saw, I thought, I believed. Can you help me with my conclusion?" This is a way to talk about a tough issue when you do not want the discussion to become a charge and defense dialog. This is not intended to be like a court session or debate class with a winner and loser. It is intended to discover truth. Truth can be dealt with when it is out in the open, and lies lose their power in the light of day.

This process is complex to explain but becomes clearer with a hypothetical example. Suppose that a wife is suspicious of her husband's loyalty because of how he talks to another woman. She initiates a conversation with him in a safe environment:

"I know Jane is single, and I saw you talking at length with her last Saturday at the soccer field. I thought it was odd that she would hold your attention like that, and it seems to me that you talk with her often. It also feels to me like you've been emotionally distant. Based on this, I have come to believe that there is an unhealthy attraction between the two of you. Can you help me with my conclusion?"

The fourth step is to interrogate the belief. The belief is the conclusion, and the purpose of interrogation is to discover truth. The goal is to work together as a husband and wife to dig into the belief, taking advantage of "best thinking practices" as a couple. Notice that there is a difference between a conclusion and an accusation. If the wife had accused her husband of having an affair this conversation would likely turn defensive or retaliatory. She would have stated her position (belief) and been responsible to defend it. He might deny her charge, defend himself against it, or blame her for it. Instead, she is honestly asking him to help prove the conclusion as either true or false.

As a husband and wife interrogate the belief it is important that each use active listening skills. That means to listen carefully to the message rather than respond to the words, and make sure you are assigning the same meaning to the words being spoken. It helps to reflect back to each other what you are hearing, gaining confidence in communication. Do not make assumptions but rather drill down until you have clarity on meaning. Share what you are hearing the other person say, and use synonyms and examples to confirm meaning.

The goal is truth. If either one becomes argumentative, defensive, or evasive it is time to end the conversation because it is no longer on point. We must get to truth and deal with it honestly because truth equals freedom.[16] Another handy evaluation tool is found in 1 Corinthians 13:4-7 which contains a condensed guide to what is and is not love. Trust can only be restored in a love-based relationship.

We often see couples attempt to restore trust by using a law-based relationship to ensure future fidelity. That might mean using filters, monitors, accountability measures, and other tools to control behavior. But control overrides a person's free will and amounts to abuse. It may change behavior for a time, but it does not lead to a change of heart, to freedom or trust. It is not a healthy partnership if a spouse has to play the role of conscience, parole officer, or junior Holy Spirit for the other.

Instead, we want to work together to discover what each believes to be true and compare that to what God says is actually true. This is the path of mind renewal and leads to transformation and maturity.[17] In love, we can overcome conflict avoidance and press in to find truth, fully believing that the outcome will be a preferable future for us, as a couple. Mutual transformation happens because the husband and wife work together so each is changed into Christ's likeness.

In our example, the wife shared her conclusion with her husband that there was an unhealthy attraction to Jane and asked for his help to interrogate that conclusion. He explains that Jane, as a single mom, has asked him for ideas and advice on parenting her preteen son. He has been trying to help her by offering a male perspective and experience as a father. This is an example of active listening because he is affirming her observations and the way she drew her conclusion, though it does not confirm her conclusion. The next step in the dialog is to dig into the emotions and beliefs that have surfaced because of these events.

This is how we act as a mirror for each other. We reflect what we see and believe so our spouse can see it from a different perspective. The goal is truth. For this reason we strive to be an accurate reflection of each other. We practice sharing observations and interpretations, while guarding against distortion from wounds or misinformation.

Suppose that the wife's intuition is correct and Jane represents an unhealthy attraction to her husband. He may not be aware of the risks inherent in this situation, and the early caution would be invaluable to him and the marriage. Since their common goal is to trust each other, the conversation could move to brainstorming about how they could help this single mom and maintain the integrity of their one-flesh relationship.

On the other hand, suppose the wife's intuition is incorrect and the husband is aware of the risks Jane poses to their marriage. Because the topic has come up in a safe environment, it allows the husband and wife to talk openly about what each is dealing with in the marriage. If there are issues, offenses, or missed expectations then they can address them. This brings the emotions and feelings out in the open so the light of truth can lead to healing.

Alternatively, suppose the wife's intuition is not correct but stems from jealousy or insecurity on her part. The conversation allows them to discuss the situation from the perspective of a one-flesh relationship. She may be triggered by the observation and responding out of emotional trauma or pain that remains from an unresolved former situation. The conversation can then lead to her healing in those areas.

Finally, suppose that the wife's intuition is correct and her husband has broken trust by having a relationship with Jane. Infidelity can be physical, emotional and/or spiritual. Suppressing the knowledge or minimizing its impact does not bring about wholeness or oneness, but allows the breach to continue to separate the husband and wife. Dealing with the truth is the only way to resolve the conflict.

In any case, the goal is to act as a mirror to each other to bring out the challenges. Love-based relating then allows for individual and mutual healing based on the confidence each of us has in the character of the Lord being reflected through our spouse.

We must begin with a humble attitude about our conclusions or risk making matters worse. Jesus taught that each should do an integrity check on his own heart before pointing out the problem in his spouse's heart. In fact, He uses an analogy of relative proportion when He describes the log in your eye compared to the speck in the other's eye.[18] We need to make sure that we are seeing clearly and that the motivations of our heart are to restore unity and oneness.

If our wounds still need to be tended it affects our reason for pointing out our spouse's "speck." We may want vengeance or pity or leverage, but each of these will cause separation between us instead of union. So we need to evaluate the intent of our heart before we attempt to take that speck out of his eye. Then we are able to move toward restoring our redeemed identity, both as individuals and as a couple.

A quick review of Chapter 4 may be in order because being forgiven, forgiving and reconciled are the key steps required before trust can be granted after a breach of any kind. We assume that the heavy lifting of forgiveness has already been done in your relationship, and that any significant offenses and breaches of trust between you have been dealt with, and that restoring trust has been made possible.

Reconciliation means that we have come to agreement on how we see things. We may begin a conversation to restore trust and feel like the differences are irreconcilable, but when our spouse shares his perspective it might clear up the differences. The conflict is resolved by additional information, something we could not see from our singular perspective. There are times where the conflict between differences cannot be resolved this way because we have drawn a false conclusion. In these cases we must reconcile our conclusion to truth. It is the only absolute standard.

Forgiveness is the only solution to differences in a relationship. Whether you call them specks or logs, these conflicts separate two people until they are reconciled to truth. Forgiving your spouse means that you release him from the offense of the conflict. It is just as important to know that you are forgiven, to receive forgiveness and no longer have feelings of guilt or debt associated with the conflict. No one can get to trust without forgiveness.

Trust grows out of forgiveness because it allows faith to replace fear. Distrust acts as a guard against further injury, but it is a fear-based protector. The opposite of fear is faith, and the object of faith is love. Trust can be restored through reconciliation because the forgiven person is a new creature, able to accurately reflect the character of God. Trust is the response to the request: "God sees me as a new creation; please agree with Him."

One challenge we see facing couples is "persistence of identity." It happens when an injured spouse is unwilling to forgive, and therefore unable to grant trust. They continue to project the old nature on their spouse, calling him or her back to that identity and demanding that he or she stay there. No amount of performance can repay the debt, nor sorrow mitigate it. It is keeping a record of wrongs instead of loving.[19]

For example, I (Calvin) have been ministering to a man that longs to have trust restored with his wife. He confessed his unfaithfulness, explored the ways he had offended her, and begged for forgiveness. He felt God's forgiveness and had restored relationship with Him, but not with his wife. She continued to hold it against him and guarded her heart with fear.

"I don't know what else to do," he said. "She doesn't trust me, and there is nothing I can do about it."

I agreed and added, "There is nothing you can do because trust has to be granted, it cannot be earned. Until she is willing to forgive you, and replace fear with faith, she will not be able to grant it to you."

His wife had fear of future pain, and fear that her husband would cause it. Healing can only come when she replaces that fear with faith; faith in his redeemed character. She identified him as unfaithful (historically accurate) and had not accepted him as a new creation.

They are stuck in separate identities instead of being merged. The conflict has functioned as a wedge between them, increasing the separation. Reconciliation would allow the conflict to be overcome by God's love and forgiveness, and it would then weld them together. Having been reunited by love, they would be able to face greater adversity together and refuse to let it divide them. The Holy Spirit's desire is always for unity, reconciliation and restoration.

A Culture of Trust

We can develop a culture of trust in our relationship, so that our frame of reference is to place prophetic confidence in our spouse's redeemed character. This is a give and receive proposition, meaning that we give prophetic confidence as well as receive it. It is an environment that encourages each to grow in their identity in Christ, and helps them by projecting truth on and in them.

Give each other the benefit of the doubt. When you doubt someone's character suspicion grows, but when you give someone the benefit of the doubt you assume the best in them first. In other words, you are doubting your assessment of the situation, rather than their character. This goes along with the humble attitude with which you communicate in that safe environment. Imagine that someone comes to you with a juicy tidbit about your spouse's possible moral failure. Rather than entertain the idea, simply state that you doubt its validity. Hold your spouse in high regard.

Give each other a reputation to live up to. Love bears all things, hopes all things, believes all things.[20] When you believe the best about your spouse, he is able to perceive himself in that same way. It affects the way you relate with each other, and speak about or to one another. There is creative power in our words and actions, so we should speak life and blessing into our relationship.

The culture of trust is demonstrated by speaking the truth in love.[21] The goal is that each person grows up in every way into Christ. This means we take consideration of the other's needs and skills with the intent that our way of talking will build each up as well as the partnership. We grow into spiritual maturity (wholeness) just like we grow into oneness: simultaneously as individuals and as a union.

The culture of trust opens the way for our home to be blessed by God. This is the desire of every Christian family, that each member be inundated with God's blessing. The love chapter (1 Corinthians 13) describes the actions and behaviors that accompany this kind of home. These traits are outcomes of the blessing and love, not the method to achieve them.

When others experience the blessings of your home, they are put face to face with the character of God.

Living in this kind of relationship causes your marriage to influence your children and grandchildren for good. Generational curses are described as having power to the third and fourth generation, but generational blessings are given to thousands of generations. Model this kind of trust relationship to your family and they will learn to trust God and each other.

Your blessed home models trust to the world. You are part of God's plan to influence the culture around you for good. Hopeless and dying people are desperate for a glimpse of the eternal love of God. Your relationship with your husband or wife may be the most tangible proof they will have of God's faithfulness, mercy, and forgiveness.

We are called to be a people that live and love differently than has ever been seen before, because the trust and love that we have is grounded in the firm foundation of God's character. Live your marriage as a testimony to the character of God.

Homework Assignments

1. Discuss together: What have I done to break trust?
2. Ask your spouse: What do I do that arouses your suspicion?
3. Take time this week to commend your spouse to another person.

End Notes

Chapter 1: Being One Flesh

[1] Mark 12:29-31 (PAR).
[2] Exodus 15:11; Psalm 113:5; Isaiah 45:18 and other places.
[3] John 1:3; Colossians 1:15-16.
[4] Isaiah 54:5.
[5] Jeremiah 2:2.
[6] Ezekiel 16..
[7] Psalm 103:13.
[8] Jeremiah 31:9; Malachi 2:10.
[9] Matthew 6:9; John 1:12-14.
[10] 2 Corinthians 3:18.
[11] Matthew 19:4-6.
[12] Ephesians 5:32.
[13] 1 Corinthians 6:17.
[14] Ephesians 5:33.
[15] Genesis 2:24.
[16] Philippians 2:2-4.
[17] Ecclesiastes 4:9-12.
[18] John 17:22-23.
[19] 1 Corinthians 2:16.
[20] Matthew 19:4-6.
[21] John 17:20-23 (NASB).
[22] Philippians 2:1-4.
[23] Ephesians 4:1-3.
[24] 1 Corinthians 7:4-5.
[25] Ephesians 5:22-32.
[26] Romans 7:18-19.
[27] Galatians 5:16-17.
[28] Romans 12:1

Chapter 2: Covenant

[1] Dan and Jody Mayhew, *Sword of Submission* (Portland: Two Worlds Press, 2011) p. 145.
[2] John 14:1-4.
[3] 1 Thessalonians 4:16.
[4] Seen on www.failblog.org
[5] Matthew 22:35-40.
[6] Matthew 5:17-28.
[7] John 13:34-35.
[8] 1 John 3:8.
[9] 1 John 4:16-19.
[10] Matthew 5:33-37.
[11] Hebrews 6:13.
[12] 1 John 1:9.
[13] John 6:63; Deuteronomy 32:47.
[14] Hebrews 9:15.
[15] Hebrews 10:9-10.
[16] John 13:34.
[17] 2 Corinthians 5:16-21.

Chapter 3: Naked and Unashamed

[1] Deuteronomy 6:4.
[2] Genesis 2:24.
[3] Genesis 2:25.
[4] Genesis 1:31.
[5] 1 Peter 3:7; Proverbs 20:29.
[6] 1 Peter 3:3; 1 Corinthians 11:15.
[7] 2 Corinthians 10:12.
[8] 1 Corinthians 12:14-20.
[9] James G. Friesen, Ph.D, et al. *The Life Model: Living from the Heart Jesus Gave You*, 2010. (Pasadena: Shepherds House).

Chapter 4: Forgiveness

[1] Romans 3:23.
[2] Romans 5:8.
[3] John 16:8-10.
[4] Revelation 12:10.
[5] Matthew 18:23-35.
[6] Genesis 3:6.
[7] 1 John 1:9.
[8] 2 Samuel 12:13; Psalm 51:3-4.
[9] Acts 26:20.
[10] Ephesians 4:28.
[11] Luke 7:40-47.
[12] Matthew 6:14-15.
[13] Matthew 18:35.
[14] 1 John 1:9.
[15] Romans 5:8.
[16] Matthew 10:8.
[17] Luke 6:37-38.
[18] Exodus 20:12.
[19] Ephesians 4:26.
[20] Luke 11:13.
[21] James 1:17.
[22] Ephesians 3:20.
[23] Psalms 55:12-14 (NET).
[24] Matthew 18:21-22 (NET).
[25] Romans 12:18.
[26] John 15:13.
[27] Romans 12:2.
[28] Genesis 2:24.
[29] 2 Corinthians 5:16.
[30] 2 Corinthians 5:17.
[31] Romans 13:8.
[32] Romans 12:18.
[33] 1 Peter 4:8.

Chapter 5: Kinds of Relating

[1] Romans 4:15 (NET).
[2] Romans 7:8 (NET).
[3] John 8:32.
[4] Romans 8:15 (NET).
[5] 2 Corinthians 3:17.
[6] Galatians 5:1 (NET).
[7] 1 John 1:9.
[8] James 4:1-8 (NASB).
[9] Ephesians 4:26.
[10] John 7:38.
[11] 2 Corinthians 12:20-21 (ESV).
[12] 1 Corinthians 7: 1-9 (ESV).
[13] Hebrews 2:14-15.
[14] Psalm 111:10; Proverbs 1:7.
[15] John 15:12-13.
[16] John 10:17-18.
[17] Ephesians 5:25-27.
[18] Romans 12:10.
[19] 1 John 4:18.

Chapter 6: Trust

[1] Hebrews 13:5; Deuteronomy 31:8; Psalm 37:28.
[2] 1 John 4:16-19.
[3] 2 Corinthians 5:17.
[4] Philippians 2:12-15.
[5] Psalm 22:9.
[6] Friesen, Wilder, et.al. *Living from the Heart Jesus Gave You* Shepherd's House, Pasadena, 2000.
[7] Romans 8:15; 2 Timothy 1:7.
[8] 2 Corinthians 10:5 (NASB).

[9] Joshua Piven; *Worst Case Scenario Survival Handbook* (Quirk Publications, 1999).

[10] Hebrews 2:14-15 (ESV).

[11] Ephesians 4:3.

[12] Romans 5:8.

[13] Genesis 2:24.

[14] Hebrews 11:1.

[15] 1 John 1:10; 1 Corinthians 10:13.

[16] John 8:32, 36.

[17] Ephesians 4:14-15.

[18] Matthew 7:3-5.

[19] 1 Corinthians 13:5.

[20] 1 Corinthians 13:7.

[21] Ephesians 4:15-16.

Resources

For more information about the concepts in this book and to order copies of Marriage Rx.

www.marriagerx.org
www.twoworldsmedia.com

The Tademas and the Mayhews may be found on the Internet. You are invited to visit the following sites:

www.mastersmindministry.org (Calvin & Julie)
www.tween2worlds.us (Dan & Jody)

31876764R00126

Made in the USA
San Bernardino, CA
22 March 2016